ENGLISH ARCHITECTURE

A MAP OF
ENGLAND
shewing some of the
NATURAL PRODUCTS
and some
CHARACTERISTICS
of
BUILDING &
ARCHITECTURE
peculiar to
DIFFERENT
LOCALITIES

SLATE & GRANITE

CARBONIFEROUS LIMESTONES & SANDSTONES

ARCHITECTURE WITH LITTLE SCULPTURE

PAINTING

MAGNESIAN LIMESTONE

OOLITE LIMESTONE

SLATE

RED SANDSTONE

WOODLAND timber

LEAD WORKS

ALABASTER WORKS

Fine timber

IRON WORKS

SCULPTURE

OOLITE LIMESTONE

Churches with fine timber belfries

CLOTH MAKING (Coventry) ETC

Churches with stone spires

CHALK DOWN

Good masonry

Churches with stone bell-cotes

THE FENS

CLOTH-MAKING

Flint work and early brick

Large churches

Rich plaster-work

WOODLAND COLOUR

Churches with wood spires

WOOL GROWING AND CLOTH MAKING
Churches with fine towers

Tile-hanging and timber-work
IRON WORKS

Newcastle
Carlisle
Durham
Ripon
Lancaster
York
Hull
Manchester
Chester
Lincoln (L)
Carnarvon
Shrewsbury
Lichfield
Leicester
Derby
Lynn
Norwich
Ely
Worcester
Warwick
Northampton
Cambridge
Ipswich
Hereford
St. Albans
Gloucester
Oxford
Guildford
London
Bristol
Wells
Guildford
Salisbury
Canterbury
Exeter
Dorchester
Lewes
Calais
Portland
Purbeck

10 0 10 20 30 40 50
Scale of miles

T.D.A.
1903

See page 162

ENGLISH ARCHITECTURE

BY

THOMAS DINHAM ATKINSON

ARCHITECT

AUTHOR OF 'A GLOSSARY OF ENGLISH ARCHITECTURE';
'ENGLISH AND WELSH CATHEDRALS'

WITH 199 ILLUSTRATIONS AND A MAP

METHUEN & CO. LTD. LONDON

36 Essex Street, Strand. W.C.2

TO

MY FATHER

First Published in April 1904
Reprinted in 1905, 1912, 1916, 1918, 1922, 1925, 1926 (enlarged),
1928, 1932, 1937, 1946 (revised) and 1948

CATALOGUE NO. 3223/U

PRINTED IN GREAT BRITAIN

PREFACE

IT will be at once apparent that this little book deals with the mere elements—with what may be called the grammar—of the vast subject of English Architecture. The great imaginative characteristics of our architecture—its æsthetic and poetical qualities (I do not speak of Gothic architecture only) its shortcomings, its reflection of national character, the influences which shaped its course and led to its alternate rise and decline—these are questions which cannot well be dealt with in the summary fashion of the following pages. The book might, in fact, be more accurately called an account of English *building* rather than of English *architecture*, if indeed it were not impossible to separate the two.

The endeavour has been, first, to trace the gradual development of our architecture so far as to enable the reader 'to discriminate the styles', as Rickman has it; that is, to recognize approximately the date of any building he may visit; and then to give some account of the plan and arrangement of particular classes of buildings

The illustrations have been drawn by myself from my own sketches, made during the last twenty years or so, except in a few instances where other sources are acknowledged. For the loan of drawings I am indebted to Professor G. Baldwin Brown, M.A., and to Mr. C. O. King. For permission to use illustrations I have to thank Mr. B. T. Batsford, Messrs. A. and C. Black, Mr. Reginald Blomfield, M.A., F.S.A., Mr. J. A. Gotch, Mr. W. H. St. John Hope, M.A.,

Messrs. Macmillan and Bowes, Mr. J. T. Mickle-thwaite, F.S.A., Messrs. Parker, Mr. C. R. Peers, M.A., F.S.A., Mr. E. S. Prior, M.A., and the respective Presidents and Councils of the Society of Antiquaries of London, of the Royal Archæological Institute, of the Cambridge Antiquarian Society, and of the Cumberland and Westmorland Antiquarian and Archæological Society.

I also very gratefully acknowledge the kindness of several friends who have helped me with the text and with the illustrations by most valuable advice and criticism, and by reading my manuscript and proofs.

T. D. A.

CAMBRIDGE,
    Christmas, 1903

PREFACE TO THE TWELFTH EDITION

FOR this edition several passages have been re-written and some minor corrections have been made.

WINCHESTER,
    Easter, 1945

INTRODUCTION

THE subject of English Architecture is so large that it will be necessary to confine the following sketch strictly within the limits—both geographical and chronological—imposed by the term. It will be impossible to attempt a review of Scottish architecture, with its strong national character and piquant French flavour, or of the art of Ireland, which in early days passed through a phase so interesting and far-reaching in its effects. So too with the work of our own country previous to Saxon times. The mighty structures of the Britons, still shrouded in mystery, and the elaborate buildings of the Romans about which we are now learning so much, are connected by so slight a thread with all that followed that the break may, for our present purpose, be considered as absolute.

It has been common to divide English medieval architecture into several distinct styles. But this is in many respects unfortunate, and, indeed, the very use of the word style, except as applied to the great periods, such as Romanesque, Gothic, and Renaissance, is apt to be misleading. The terms Early English, Decorated, and Perpendicular are now too well established to be disregarded, but their use, if it does not actually convey an idea of definite breaks in the continuity of the art, at least suggests very rapid change from one style to another through short periods of transition. This, however, was not so. Medieval architecture was always in a period of transition. It was an unwritten law based solely upon precedent, a purely traditional art learned only at the bench, and as such it was continually advancing.

With the Renaissance the case is somewhat different. That period was not, as regards architecture, one of growth and development of at all the same kind as were the Middle Ages, neither was the art in its earlier phases vernacular in the same sense that medieval art had been. Though Renaissance architecture gave as great opportunities for variety of treatment and for originality of the highest order, its progress and development were modified by the fact that the forms in which it was expressed had become in a great degree stereotyped. New combinations and new themes were always open to the artist, but the language in which he expressed himself was scarcely so flexible as the medieval tongue; for our Renaissance architecture was based on that of the Italian masters of the fifteenth and sixteenth centuries, who took as their models the architecture of ancient Rome, which in its turn had been derived from that of Athens. That is as far as the pedigree has been traced with certainty. Greek architecture as we know it—the architecture of the great period of Greek art—was perhaps itself a renaissance, a revival of types which had had their period of struggle and growth in some still buried past. When we first meet Greek architecture it is full blown. Further refinements of extraordinary subtilty were yet to be made, but the types or orders are fixed, and are deliberately adopted. The style, eclectic and perhaps exotic, is quite developed, and requires only that perfecting for which the genius of the Greek was so eminently fitted. From the types which he perfected no serious departure has ever been made.

Besides this contrast between the rapid growth of the Western style and the unvarying types of the East, there is the great change in the conditions under which English architecture was produced after the coming of Inigo Jones. In a work of the Middle Ages much was left to the initiative and traditional methods of the craftsmen.

> 'For in the lond ther nas no crafty man,
> That geometrye or arsmetrike can,
> Ne portreyour, ne kervere of ymages,
> That Theseus ne gaf hem mete and wages
> The theatre for to maken and devyse.'

But from the beginning of the seventeenth century architecture was a matter for architects.

These facts become apparent as the narrative proceeds, and involve a different treatment of the subject. In the Middle Ages there is incessant change of form in every detail, but the personal element, or at least any proper name, is almost invariably absent. Since Renaissance times the change in details may be told in a few lines, and history is apt to become a purely critical review with a list of architects and their works.

The manner of Inigo Jones and of Wren did, however, in course of time become traditional, and many are the seventeenth- and eighteenth-century houses, the work evidently of the local builder, which we of to-day would fain copy to the best of our ability. Meanwhile the work of the architects deteriorated from various causes till it reached such a pompous dullness combined with inanity of decoration as to make the Gothic Revival inevitable. In is in this connexion that the half-prophetic remark of Campbell, in his *Vitruvius Britannicus* (written in 1715), becomes of interest. Speaking of the state of architecture in Italy, he says: 'With him [Palladio] the great manner and exquisite Taste of Building is lost; for the *Italians* can no more now relish the Antique Simplicity, but are entirely employed in capricious Ornaments, which must at last end in the *Gothic*.' The capricious ornaments which, soon after this was written, began to appear in English architecture, did at last end in the Gothic Revival with all its strange productions.

One result of this extraordinary movement has been the 'restoration' of our medieval buildings. It is impossible to leave this subject without a protest against the mutilation which too often passes under the name.

There can never be absolute agreement on the treatment of old buildings, any more than on any other question; but the general opinion among those who have given most attention to the subject is becoming more and more in favour of a very strong conservatism, and is slowly, very slowly, leavening the lump of public opinion. We are still living in an age (for indeed hardly a decade has passed) which saw the destruction of great quantities of fifteenth-century work in one of our noblest buildings to make room for modern reproductions of the original Norman and Early English; while in another case it was seriously proposed to pull down a building by Wren in order to replace it by one of modern Gothic. The Jacobean Communion table and the Georgian font, sanctified by the devotion of generations, are even now condemned as unsuitable. This is, of course, restoration in its crudest form, but it is still far from uncommon.

But though instances of restoration of the most

revolutionary sort still occur, most of the damage which is now done is through excessive and injudicious repair. Every stone which shows signs of decay or has been chipped, is cut out. Maybe it has taken six or eight hundred years to effect this slight degree of damage, and there is therefore presumably yet a good deal of life before it. Every bit of red brick with which a stone building has been repaired is cut out, especially if it be in a church, for it is not thought to be an 'ecclesiastical' material, though these patches are often of excellent workmanship, and their warm colour always makes a delightful harmony with the grey stone. The old patchwork pavement is changed for monotonous red tiles. The screenwork, which has generally been covered with brown paint, retains under this the medieval decoration of gilding and colour, but the acids which are applied remove not only the modern oil paint, but often also the medieval colouring, and the work is put up again with a brown, woolly surface, which would have horrified the original builders. The plaster is stripped off the roughest rubble walls, sometimes even inside as well as outside—a measure generally disastrous to the building æsthetically and very far removed from the ancient practice; for the medieval builders almost always covered their walls, even when built of good masonry, with plaster of exquisite fineness, which they whitewashed if they did not decorate it with colour.

The lines on which the treatment of old buildings should proceed may be briefly laid down thus: No object should be destroyed because it is in a style which we happen to dislike; the structural parts should be repaired in the best possible way, but no attempt should be made to restore decorative features; alterations should only be made where absolutely necessary for practical reasons; new work should honestly, though not ostentatiously, show itself as such; beauty should not be sacrificed to such mistaken notions of archæology as, for instance, that all constructive features and materials ought to be left exposed to view; nor, on the other hand, should history and association be wantonly sacrificed to what we consider beautiful.

In conclusion, I may mention a few books which have been very useful to me and will be useful to others. Unfortunately architectural literature, although considerable in bulk, was for a long time unscientific in its methods and limited in its range. In the field of medieval architecture there was too much theory and not enough minute and systematic recording of facts; in works on classical architecture there has been a tendency merely to describe particular buildings, without any attempt at a connected general history; and it may be said that until the last few years a reasonable account of Renaissance architecture did not exist. There is still no general work on Roman architecture in England or on conventual buildings. A knowledge of either subject has to be gleaned from scattered papers in the publications of archæological societies, those on the latter subject by Sir William St. John Hope being especially valuable.

The foundations of intelligent architectural history were laid by Thomas Rickman in his *Attempt to Discriminate the Styles of Architecture in England from the Conquest to the Reformation,* published in 1817. This has been several times re-edited and enlarged by John Henry Parker, who added many excellent illustrations and a useful list of dated examples. Mr. Parker also published the invaluable *Glossary of Terms used in Grecian, Roman, Italian, and Gothic Architecture* (3 vols. 8vo. Oxford, 1850; out of print), *A Concise Glossary* (1 vol. sm. 8vo, 1879, 7s. 6d.), and *An Introduction to the Study of Gothic Architecture*, besides other works.

Professor J. Fergusson's general *History* in six volumes (8vo. 1893–1910) includes every land, and is most valuable.

On church architecture in particular there is M. H. Bloxam's *Principles of Gothic Ecclesiastical Architecture* (2 vols. 8 vo, 11th edition, 1882), which is excellent, though it scarcely deals with 'principles'. The third volume is called *A Companion to Gothic Architecture*, and was reissued separately in 1903 as *Essays on Church Vestments*, etc., at 3s. 6d. George Gilbert Scott, the son of Sir Gilbert (whose *Lectures* are rather for those intending to enter the profession), wrote the learned, and very discursive work, *An Essay on the History of English Church Architecture* (4to, 1881).

Development and Character of Gothic Architecture, by Professor C. H. Moore, of Cambridge, Mass. (8vo. London, 2nd ed., 1899), is a purely critical work on the principles of Gothic architecture, written with considerable power, to show that the Gothic style was never fully developed in any country but France. Professor Moore's *Mediæval Church Architecture in England* (8vo, 1912, 15s.) should also be read. A *History of Gothic Art in England*, by Professor Prior, A.R.A. (8vo. 1900, 31s. 6d.), an original and valuable work, is a critical appreciation of the national style in its local and other variations. In their excellent *An Acccount of Medieval Figure*

Sculpture in England, Professor Prior and Mr. A. Gardner (4to, 1912) break new ground. Mr. Francis Bond's two large works, *Gothic Architecture in England* (imp. 8vo, 1905, 31*s*. 6*d*.) and *An Introduction to English Church Architecture* (2 vols. 4to, 1913. 42*s*.), and his small monographs on *Fonts and Font Covers*, on *Stalls and Tabernacle Work*, and on *Screens and Galleries* (6*s*. each), are all useful.

For Saxon architecture *Arts in Early England* (2 vols., 1903, 32*s*.) of Professor Baldwin Brown should be consulted, and also the pages of the *Archæological Journal*, especially Mr. J. T. Micklethwaite's valuable paper, 'Something about Saxon Church Building' (vol. liii, 1896).

On the subject of medieval houses, *Some Account of Domestic Architecture in England from the Conquest to the time of Henry VIII*, by T. Hudson Turner and J. H. Parker (4 vols. 8vo. Parker: 1851–9, out of print) is a store of useful material. Mr. J. A. Gotch's *Growth of the English House* (8vo, 1909, 7*s*. 6*d*.) should be read. On the kindred subject of collegiate architecture there is the great *Architectural History of the University and Colleges of Cambridge*, by Professor R. Willis and J. W. Clark (4 vols. 8vo. Cambridge, 1886, £4 4*s*.). They have drawn up the ladder after them. The same remark applies to Mr. Clark's work on library buildings and fittings, *The Care of Books* (8vo, 1901). *Mediæval Military Architecture in England*, by G. T. Clark (2 vols. 8vo. Wyman, 1884) is the standard work on castles, although the author's views as to origins cannot now be accepted in the light of recent research. The student should consult Mr. A. H. Thompson's *Military Architecture in England* (8vo. Oxford, 1912, 7*s*. 6*d*.).

There are many good books on other special branches of the subject. *The Rites of Durham* gives a vivid and detailed account of the church and its furniture, the conventual buildings, and the monastic life, written by one of the monks after the suppression of the monastery (8vo. Surtees Society, 1842; new edition with plan, 1903). Abbot Gasquet's *English Monastic Life* (8vo, 1904, 10s. 6d.) gives some account of the buildings, has some excellent plans, and a useful list of all the known religious houses. Mr. Micklethwaite's *Ornaments of the Rubric* and Sir W. St. J. Hope's *English Altar* (both Alcuin Club publications), and *English Church Furniture*, by Dr. J. C. Cox and Mr. A. Harvey (8vo, 1907, 10s. 6d.), are the most authoritative works on those subjects. A good account of church vestments is given in Professor Macalister's *Ecclesiastical Vestments* (8vo, 1896, 6s.) and in a number of other works. Cardwell's *Documentary Annals of the Reformed Church of England* (2 vols. 8vo, 1844) is the authority for the changes of the sixteenth and seventeenth centuries. Bloxam's *Companion*, mentioned above, deals with the subject. *Roodscreens and Roodlofts* by Mr. F. B. Bond and the Rev. Dom Bede Camm (2 vols. 4to, 1909, 32s.) is the most important work on the subject.

R. and J. A. Brandon's *Open Timber Roofs of the Middle Ages* (4to, London, 1849) contains excellent drawings, but is out of print. *The Archæological Journal* for 1914 contains a valuable paper on the subject by Mr. F. E. Howard. F. A. Paley's *Manual of Gothic Moldings* (8vo, 6th edition, 1902, 7s. 6d.) gives a very large and admirable collection of sections, without, however, sufficient indication of their scale and construction and what may be

called their context. Professor Willis's papers on
the 'Vaults of the Middle Ages' (*Trans. Ryl. Inst. of
Brit. Archts.*, vol. i, part ii, 1842) still forms the
best text-book on the subject; perhaps a like remark
applies to all his architectural writings. Mr. Howard's
paper on 'Fan Vaulting' in *The Archæological
Journal* for 1911 must also be studied. Mr. J.
Starkie Gardner's *Ironwork* (2 vols. 8vo, 6s. South
Kensington Mus. Art Handbks., 1893) and Professor W. R. Lethaby's *Leadwork* (8vo, 1893,
4s. 6d.) are handy and authoritative.

During the eighteenth century a number of large
works on contemporary architecture were published,
but Colin Campbell's *Vitruvius Britannicus*[1] is the
only one of general interest. This is a valuable work.
consisting of large engravings, with a short note on
each, but with no text. It is very far from im-
partial, the selection displaying the usual animus
against Wren. It should be explained that the
books of this period which profess to illustrate the
work of Inigo Jones attribute to him a large number
of designs which are really the work of others.[2]

As might be expected, little was produced on the
subject of Renaissance architecture during the
nineteenth century until near its close. But in 1897
Professor Blomfield, A.R.A., published his *History
of Renaissance Architecture in England*, 1500–1800
(2 vols. 8vo, 50s.), which the reader will find to be
all that can be desired, both in matter and in manner.
To it I am particularly indebted. Professor Blomfield has condensed it into one small volume in his
Short History (large cr. 8vo, 1900, 7s. 6d.).

[1] Fol., vols. i, ii, 1715; vol. iii, 1725, continued by Woolfe
and Gandon (vols. iv, v), 1767–71, and under the title *New
Vitruvius Britannicus*, by Richardson (vols. vi, vii), 1802–8.
[2] Blomfield.

There are several large works on special phases of the Renaissance, which, though not really dear, are rather expensive, such as Mr. Gotch's *Architecture of the Renaissance in England,* 1560–1635 (2 vols. fol., 1894, £8 8*s.*), and Messrs. Belcher and Macartney's *Later Renaissance Architecture in England* (2 vols. fol., 1901, £8 8*s.*). These are illustrative works, with short descriptive text. Mr. Gotch has issued a smaller work on the same period (8vo, 21*s.*), and it is to be hoped that Mr. Macartney will follow his example. Messrs. H. Inigo Triggs and H. Tanner have published *Some Architectural Works of Inigo Jones* (fol., 30*s.*), and Mr. G. H. Birch, *London Churches of the XVIIth and XVIIIth Centuries* (fol., £4 4*s.*).

It will be understood that this short list professes to indicate but a selection of the works on the subject and of those on the historical side only; it includes none of the excellent appreciations of English Architecture in its artistic aspect.

But however delightful books may be, and necessary as they are in some branches of the art, the true way to study architecture, the only really satisfactory way, and by far the most attractive, is the close examination of the buildings themselves.

CONTENTS

ILLUSTRATIONS

Map of England, showing some of the natural products and some characteristics of Building and Architecture peculiar to different localities *Frontispiece*

CHAPTER I
ROMANESQUE

xix

CHAPTER II

GOTHIC

EARLY ENGLISH

CHAPTER III

RENAISSANCE

TUDOR

STUART

CHAPTER IV
CHURCHES

CHAPTER V

MONASTERIES

CHAPTER VI

HOUSES

CHAPTER VII

CONCLUSION

APPENDIX

THE NINETEENTH CENTURY

GLOSSARY

CHAPTER I
ROMANESQUE

SAXON

THE Saxons were but little influenced by those
Roman buildings which had survived the troubled
interval between the departure of the legions and
their own settlement in the land. Their houses
seem to have been generally of wood, ornamented
with rude carvings and covered with thatch or with
shingles. They consisted usually of one room; only
the greater houses seem to have had a second room
as a sleeping place for the thane and his family
and the more honoured guests. But in the south of
England at least the earliest builders (namely, those
of the seventh and eighth centuries) tried to copy
the style and technique of the Romans, and they no
doubt used to some extent materials from ruined
Roman buildings, such as the large thin Roman
bricks. The Saxons seem to have had some of the
Roman skill in building and were consequently able
to make their walls thin. In this respect they
contrast strongly with Normans, whose work is

1

so often of excessive massiveness and of inferior quality.

No buildings other than churches now remain.

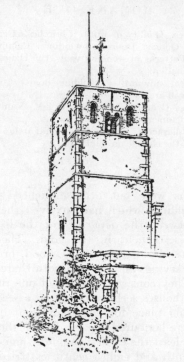

FIG. 1. TOWER OF ST BENEDICT'S CHURCH, CAMBRIDGE
PROBABLY EARLY ELEVENTH CENTURY

But churches of which the whole or a considerable part are Saxon are fairly numerous and of great interest. Their ritual arrangement will be noticed in a later chapter; it will be, therefore, only necessary here to describe their architectural features and methods of construction.

During the Saxon period architecture seems to have deteriorated.[1] The Danish invasions would amply account for this. Most of the features usually recognized as characteristic of the style, belong only to the latest buildings, that is, to those of the tenth and eleventh centuries.

The towers are usually tall and thin. They are divided into stages of about equal height by a series of offsets, each stage being rather narrower than the one below it. The belfry windows have a strongly marked character of their own. They are divided by balluster-shaped columns set in the middle of the wall, and supporting a long stone running from inside to outside to carry the arches.

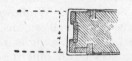

FIG. 2. ROMAN BRICKS AND SLAB CONSTRUCTION

ARCHWAY AND PLAN OF ONE PIER BRITFORD CHURCH

Thus the Saxon towers strongly resemble those of the early churches in Rome, by which they were no doubt largely influenced, They were probably surmounted by a low pyramidal spire of stone or wood, or by a roof with a gable over each face of the tower.[2] The balluster-shafts were copied from

[1] J. T. Micklethwaite.   [2] Sompting (Fig. 3).

Roman work, and were used in other parts besides the towers. Arches are always round and of a single ring; door jambs are not splayed or rebated; windows are small, and in the early churches are splayed on the inside; buttresses are very rarely used at the angles or elsewhere.

In late work the angles are built in what is known as 'long-and-short' work, that is, with flat slabs alternating with tall pillar-like stones. In the earliest Saxon work, as in post-Conquest work, all the quoins are the same height, all have one side longer than the other, like a brick, and the long sides are placed alternately on each side of the building.

The doors and windows have usually round arches, or a small window has a semicircular head cut in a single stone,[1] and not infrequently the windows are complete circles. Sometimes a triangular head is formed over a door by two large stones leaning against one another;[2] a plain lintel is never used. Windows, in late work, are splayed outside as well as inside, so that the narrowest part of the opening is in the middle of the wall.[3] In the very latest buildings there is once more a splay on the inside only, but this is probably due to Norman influence.

Columns are round, and are sometimes ornamented with vertical or spiral flutings,[4] or they are balluster-shaped, and are spoken of as 'turned'. The capitals are rudely sculptured and have a chamfered or moulded abacus. The arches are round and of one 'order',[5] which is plain or moulded on the face only. Barrel vaults were used over small spans.

[1] Fig. 5.   [2] Deerhurst, Gloster; Barnack, Northants.
[3] Fig. 6.   [4] Deerhurst.   [5] See Glossary and Fig. 2.

A remarkable feature in buildings of the tenth and eleventh centuries is the pattern formed on the face of a wall by narrow vertical strips of stone,

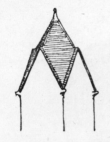

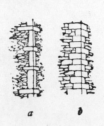

FIG. 3. TOP OF TOWER
SOMPTING CHURCH

FIG. 4. QUOINS
a, LONG AND SHORT. *b*, ORDINARY

with some diagonal and arch-shaped pieces.[1] It is rather suggestive of wood-framing, and is thought by some to be derived from timber buildings; it is highly probable that this kind of work, and also

FIG. 5
SAXON WINDOW

EARLY
FIG. 6

LATE
FIG. 7

PLANS OF SAXON WINDOWS

the long-and-short quoins, are Danish rather than Saxon features.[2] Others think it more probable that the system is a rude imitation of the pilasters and entablatures of the Romans. But it occurs in the buildings erected after the incursions of the

[1] Earls Barton (Fig. 8).
[2] H. C. Windley, *Jour. R.I.B.A.*, 3rd Ser. vii, 157.

Danes, a race more familiar with timber-work than with masonry, and not in the buildings which are nearer in date to the Roman occupation.

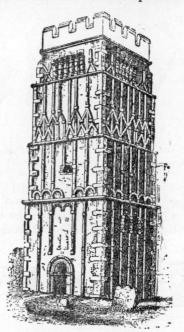

FIG. 8. TOWER OF EARLS BARTON CHURCH
PROBABLY ELEVENTH CENTURY
From Parker's 'Glossary'

The rubble walling was without a doubt plastered inside and outside. Roofs were most likely covered with thatch or with oak shingles, though it is possible that tiles were made. Glass windows were not unknown, though they probably numbered but one in ten thousand.

NORMAN

The Norman Conquest was at once followed by an extraordinary outburst of activity in building; perhaps the greatest the country has ever known. The churches of the religious houses were laid out on the grandest scale; a large number —probably the greater number —of our parish churches bear evidence of having been rebuilt at this time; many castles of great size were erected, and many others were strengthened, to hold the conquered country, while not a few substantial private houses built of stone still remain.[1]

FIG. 9. WALL ARCADES, ELY. *c.* 1170

The walls are of great thickness. At first they are built of rough rubble, or of squared stone with very thick joints (sometimes more than an inch thick), but later the work improves and the joints are much finer. In early buildings Roman bricks are still occasionally used.

The building is often enriched by a row of small arches carried on detached shafts, and in elaborate work the whole wall is covered with arcades of various designs. There are sometimes overhanging eaves, sometimes a parapet. The parapet projects about six inches beyond the face of the wall, and is carried by a corbel-table or row of grotesquely

[1] Fig. 158.

carved corbels a foot or two apart, with lintels or arches from one to another. A similar corbel-table is sometimes found under the eaves where they overhang, but perhaps all these originally carried parapets.

Buttresses are very wide, but they are of such slight projection, only a few inches, as to be of no structural use. They terminate in a gable or in a lean-to, or they run up to and stop against the

FIG. 10. CORBEL-TABLE, ELY. *c.* 1200

projecting corbel-table under the parapet. The angles of the buttresses and of the building itself are often ornamented with a shaft or small column worked on the quoins.

Doorways, especially of churches, are often very highly decorated. The jambs consist of a series of recesses with a small shaft, generally worked on the same stones as the jamb, in each recess. The head of the doorway is generally a round arch, recessed like the jamb, and enriched with a great variety of ornaments; occasionally the innermost order of the arch is trefoil in form. Sometimes a lintel is used, with a corbel under each end and a relieving arch over it, the tympanum or space between the lintel and arch being filled with sculpture (Fig. 26).

Windows are treated in the same manner as doorways, but though there are some rich examples, they are generally comparatively plain, and they are almost always arched. Circular windows are also used, especially in the gables of large buildings.

The columns, though exceedingly massive, have

merely a facing of ashlar with a core of rubble.
This method of building requires good mortar, and
Norman mortar was generally very bad. In plan
they are usually round, or else they are square with

FIG. 11. SOUTH-EAST DOOR, ELY. *c.* 1150

a series of recesses at the angles and with half
columns on the faces; they occasionally have spiral
or zigzag flutings. The bases are low and insignificant.
The two component parts of a capital, the bell or
capital proper and the abacus, are, in Norman
work, formed of separate stones. In plan, the
abacus of a large pier generally follows approximately the plan of the pier itself; for small shafts it

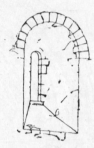

FIG. 12. WINDOW IN
STOURBRIDGE CHAPEL,
CAMBRIDGE. *c.* 1150

FIG. 13. INTERIOR OF
AN EARLY NORMAN
WINDOW

is invariably square, and is so occasionally even for
large round columns. In profile the upper edge is a
right angle, differing in this respect from all later
forms, and the lower edge is chamfered. The lower
part of the capital is made round to fit the column,
while the upper part is square to fit the abacus.
The result is known as the 'cushion capital'. This in
its simplest form is the commonest Norman capital,
and is the parent of some of the more elaborate
sorts. The most common way of decorating this
plain block of stone is by cutting vertical flutes,
producing what is called the 'scolloped capital',
from its resemblance to a scallop shell. Another

FIG. 14. NORTH-EAST TRANSEPT, CANTERBURY. 1174

form used for small capitals towards the end of the
period, has four leaves springing from the neck and
bending over under the angles of the square part
and ending in volutes.[1] Other varieties have a rude

[1] Figs. 19, 20.

imitation of the more orthodox volute; some are of the cushion form but are covered with surface carving.[1] In the latter part of the twelfth century many capitals are carved with genuine foliage springing upwards from the neck of the capital and curling over under the abacus. Occasionally, in its

FIG. 15. CUSHION CAPITAL.

FIG. 16. SCOLLOP CAPITAL

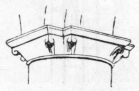

FIG. 17. CAPITAL WITH
VOLUTES, ELY. *c.* 1090

FIG. 18. SCOLLOP CAPITAL,
ELY. *c.* 1140

general symmetrical arrangement and also in the character of the leaves, the Norman capital of this class resembles the acanthus capital of the Roman Corinthian order, from which it was ultimately derived. The edges of the leaves are deeply serrated, and the leaves under the projecting angle of the square abacus have a volute-like form. This derivation from the classical acanthus is an important link in the history of art. But most examples show a departure from the acanthus form. The serrations are omitted, and the volute becomes

[1] Fig. 11.

a knob of opening foliage. Before very long the
knob did open in a most interesting way, as will be
described on a later page.

The arches are round, sometimes stilted, or
even slightly horseshoe-shaped. They are generally

FIG. 19. REVERSED VOLUTES,
BUILDWAS. *c.* 1160

FIG. 20. REVERSED VOLUTES,
ST. MARY'S CHURCH,
SHREWSBURY. *c.* 1160.

FIG. 21. ACANTHUS-LIKE
FOLIAGE, ST. CROSS.
c. 1160

built of several 'orders' or concentric rings of
voussoirs, each order being recessed somewhat
farther back from the face of the wall than that
above it.[1] Small arches, as of doors, windows, and
wall arcades, are generally more richly ornamented
than large arches.

Small buildings are sometimes covered with a

[1] Fig. 24.

barrel vault. More commonly the aisles of a church
have groined vaulting[1] and the nave a wooden roof
only; the early builders were daunted by the height
and width of the nave; the north transept of Durham,
about 1100, is an exceptionally early example of a
large vault. The early groined vaults have only

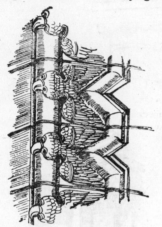

FIG. 22. BIRD'S-BEAK   FIG. 23. SECTION OF ARCH,
ENRICHMENT, ST. CROSS.   ST. BARTHOLOMEW'S,
c. 1150   SMITHFIELD. 1133

transverse ribs, but about 1100 diagonal ribs are
added. Now these diagonal ribs being much longer
than the transverse ribs, they rose, if both were
made semicircular, to a greater height. This produced inconvenient forms in the spandrels, and
various expedients were resorted to, such as stilting
the transverse arches and depressing the diagonals,
in order to make the crowns of the two more nearly
at the same level.

[1] If vaulted at all.

The mouldings are few and simple, the enrichments various and elaborate. The hood-mould of
the arch, in this as in succeeding styles is generally
similar to the abacus of the capital. Arch-moulds
are bold rolls and shallow hollows. The commonest
enrichments are the shallow zigzag and the billet,

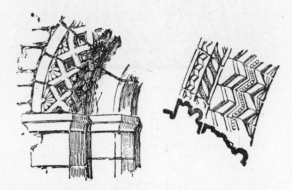

FIG. 24. IMPOST AND ARCH,   FIG. 25. ENRICHMENTS OF
ALSOP-IN-THE-DALE   ARCH, ST. CROSS

used on string courses and arches; the rich and bold
chevron, and the weird bird's-beak, used on arches
only. The sculpture is shallow, the parts in relief
being flat, like the ground, so that the effect is
produced by broad level surfaces and lines rather
than by true modelling.

Few, if any, roofs remain, but there can be no
doubt that they had level tie-beams, and that each
pair of rafters was framed together by cross pieces,
forming what is called a 'trussed rafter' roof (see p.
31). The pitch was moderately steep, and there was
often a level boarded ceiling.

FIG. 26. SCULPTURED TYMPANUM, ELY. *c.* 1140

TRANSITION

During the third quarter of the twelfth century new features and new methods began to be introduced. The work becomes more refined, the walls and columns are thinner, the carving more delicate. The chisel was used more commonly than in early times and the axe less often. But the change was very gradual, and features belonging to the Norman style and to that which succeeded it are found side by side in work of this period of transition. Pointed arches are enriched with Norman ornaments, and supported on columns of the massive Norman proportions. Old forms are sometimes clung to while the technique improves; or, on the other hand, the newer fashions are adopted while the skill to carry them out is wanting.

The most important change is that from the round to the pointed arch. Many baseless theories as to the origin of the latter form have been put forward, as, for instance, that it was suggested by the intersecting round arches common in Norman work,[1] by the *vesica piscis* or 'glory' of pointed oval form,[2] and so on. But the pointed arch had

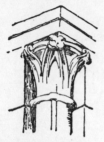

FIG. 27. CAPITAL
ST. MARY'S, SHREWS-
BURY. *c.* 1180

FIG. 28. CAPITAL,
ST. MARY'S SHREWSBURY,
c. 1180

been long employed constructionally in the East, and had gradually spread westward and northward. It was used by the Mohammedans, and was probably introduced by them into Sicily and other countries which they conquered in the eighth and ninth centuries. It is found in the south of France early in the eleventh century, but not in the north till at least a hundred years later. It was in use in England in the first half of the twelfth century. The Cistercians were among the first to adopt it, and they were using it freely by 1150. Their earliest houses in England had been founded about twenty years before, and in these the first buildings have

[1] Fig. 9.   [2] Fig. 26.

round arches. The Benedictines used it in the nave vault of Durham in 1130.

It seems that in several countries, both in the East and West, the adoption of the pointed arch was due to constructional considerations; it was its structural quality that recommended it in England, for with its introduction the chief difficulties of vaulting vanished (see p. 28).

FIG. 20. CAPITAL,
ST. MARY'S, SHREWSBURY,
c. 1180

CHAPTER II

GOTHIC

EARLY ENGLISH: King Henry III. Contrast with Norman.
Quality of masonry. Windows. Doors. Buttresses.
Columns. Capitals, foliage, Bases. Annulets. Arches.
Mouldings. Vaulting. Roofs.

DECORATED: The development of tracery, geometrical,
flowing. Foliage. Columns. Mouldings. Ogee-arches.
Vaults. Roofs.

PERPENDICULAR: Reduction of wall surface. Windows.
Doorways. Buttresses. Columns. Arches. mouldings.
Foliage. Enrichments. Panelling in stonework. Vault-
ing. Roofs.

EARLY ENGLISH

BY the end of the twelfth century Gothic architecture had established itself as a distinct style; that is
to say, it had cast off the last traces of Romanesque.
Church building, to which, during the twelfth
century, the architectural energy of the people had
been devoted, had received a severe check by the
sixteen years' interdict of King John's reign.[1] But
soon after the accession in 1216 of Henry III, who
was himself an enthusiast, architecture revived and
developed with extraordinary rapidity. Henry began
Westminster Abbey in 1245.[2] The century which
followed is the great period of English art.

Massive construction had given way to extreme
lightness, and instead of the general squareness of
Norman proportion, height is increased and emphasis
is given to the vertical line.

The quality of the masonry continued to improve

[1] This statement is disputed by some good authorities.
[2] He began the Lady Chapel, now destroyed, in 1220.

till it reached a high degree of perfection. The comparative simplicity of the style did not present the complicated problems of the later work, but for accuracy in setting-out and skill in workmanship,

FIG. 30. LANCETS, ST. MARY'S, SHREWSBURY.
c. 1180

the masonry of the thirteenth century has never
been surpassed.

The long, narrow lancet windows are the well-
known characteristic of the Early English style.
Their height is commonly six times their width, and
not seldom as much as ten times. In their grouping
the greatest skill is shown. Along the side of a building they are in couples, or they form a row, evenly

FIG. 31. UNPIERCED
NORMAN TYMPANUM

FIG. 32. PLATE TRACERY,
JESUS COLLEGE, CAMBRIDGE

spaced and of equal height. In a gable end or in the
clearstory of the larger churches they are in groups
of three or five, increasing in height towards the
centre, the spaces between them being often filled
with blind arches. The jambs, especially inside,
have rich clusters of thin shafts of Purbeck marble.
The glass is set near the outer face of the wall; the
inner jamb is widely splayed, but the soffit of the
arch is level.

When two lancets are embraced under one arch,
the thin wall above the lancets and below the arch
is sometimes pierced by a circle or quatrefoil. This
had been already done in the Norman triforium
arcade. The beauty of the arrangement was at once
apparent, and the idea was rapidly developed.

Externally the group was included under one hood-mould, and the piercings were enlarged. This important step, producing what is known as 'plate-tracery,' was made during the first half of the thirteenth century. From plate-tracery is derived all the tracery of later times.

Doors are generally richly moulded, and the jamb has one or more detached nook-shafts, but they are

not often treated so elaborately as in Norman buildings. The head is commonly arched; only very occasionally are a lintel and relieving arch used.

The form of buttress now used makes it possible to reduce the thickness of the wall, and at the same time it gives a more pronounced vertical line than the Norman pilaster. It has a much greater projection and less width, the two dimensions being generally nearly equal. It is diminished by offsets, and terminates near the top of the wall by a plain weathering or by a gablet, or it is carried up above the parapet and finished with a pinnacle. The angles are frequently chamfered. The corner of a building has a pair of buttresses at right angles to the walls, never one placed diagonally. When a vaulted nave rises above an aisle the thrust of the nave vault is met by flying-buttresses carried over the roof of the aisle.

FIG. 33. CLEAR-STORY WINDOW, BOURN. *c.* 1200

Columns are very slender, and are built of large blocks of dressed stone, instead of as heretofore a facing of ashlar, with a rubble core. They are generally round; in the nave arcade of a church round and octagonal columns are frequently used alternately. Sometimes they consist of four semicircles, and in the

more important buildings four or
more slender shafts of Purbeck
marble are placed round a circular
column of stone.

The capitals are of two varieties:
moulded and carved. The abacus is
worked on the same stone as the rest
of the capital; it is never square on
plan, the upper edge is always
rounded, and it is deeply undercut.
The other mouldings of the capital
are few and simple, and project
boldly from a vertical 'bell'.

FIG. 34. EARLY
ENGLISH PIERS

Before the end of the twelfth century the carved
foliage had attained the essential characteristics
which were to make it one of the chief glories of our
architecture. Some examples retain a likeness to

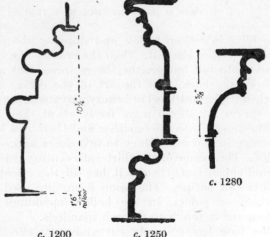

c. 1200   c. 1250

c. 1280

FIG. 35 MOULDED CAPITALS AND BASES

the parent acanthus. The commoner form is the simple leaf without serrations; it clings closely to the bell of the capital, pushing out a tight knot under the abacus or splitting into three lobes. As the knot develops the lower part of the leaf is neglected; only its central rib remains, or it becomes broad and flat with a strong rib, which reappears in the central

FIG. 36. CAPITAL, BERKLEY CHURCH. *c.* 1250

lobe lying in a deep hollow and stopping abruptly near the end of the leaf. Then the crocket-like bud breaks into full foliage, the leaves spread out and turn crisply back, and the art of the carver has reached its highest level of beauty and strength. As the sprays are tossed more freely about they are apt to mingle with one another and there is a loss of strength, and a tendency to luxuriance and confusion. The foliage of the thirteenth century copied no individual leaf, though it has all the essential qualities of nature. The same forms are used as crockets on gables, in the hollow mouldings of arches, and in scrolls to fill arch spandrels.

The base has a deeply cut and very effective moulding, derived from the Attic base. It is

sometimes called the 'water-holding moulding',
because the deep channel holds the rain-water.

FIG. 38. FOLIAGE OF
THIRTEENTH CENTURY

FIG. 37. SCROLL IN
DOOR-JAMB, WESTMINSTER.
c. 1250

FIG. 39. BAND OF FOLIAGE
ON CORBEL,
CHESTER CATHEDRAL

When a round base stands on a square or octagonal
plinth, the angle is filled by a 'spur' of foliage.

When Purbeck marble shafts are used, they are
connected with the main
column by one or more
annulets, which have
mouldings of similar character to the capital.

The arch varies in form
from a very blunt to a very
sharp point. The earliest
pointed arches had gener-
ally been blunt, but after

FIG. 40. THE SPUR OF AN
OCTAGONAL BASE,
WESTMINSTER. c. 1250

the middle of the twelfth century the shape is no guide to date. The trefoil arch had been used by the Normans, and now becomes common. The whole arch follows the trefoil form; the plain arch with a distinct cusp is a somewhat later development.

FIG. 41.   TREFOIL ARCH, WESTMINSTER.   *c.* 1250

The orders, or rings of the arch, are at first well marked, and the mouldings are very simple and bold—generally plain rolls with deep hollows. They are worked on the face and soffit of the stone, with a large roll at the angle, so that the recessed arrangement of the orders is well preserved. One of the hollows is frequently filled with the beautiful dog-tooth ornament—the one enrichment[1] of the style —or sometimes with a succession of separate leaves, or with a continuous scroll of foliage. The inner face of a wall is often, especially in churches, decorated with a diaper pattern, giving a very rich effect.

[1] See Glossary.

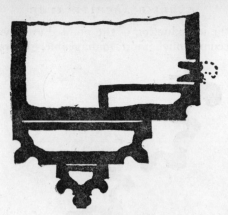

FIG. 42. SECTION OF ARCH-MOULD
THE RINGS WELL MARKED. *c.* 1180

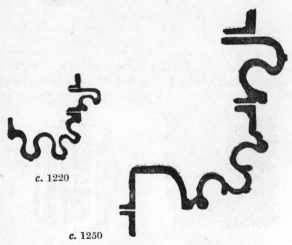

c. 1220

c. 1250

FIG. 43. SECTIONS OF ARCH-MOULDS

By the introduction of the pointed arch, vaulting had become much more manageable. It was now

FIG. 44. SECTION OF ARCH-MOULD
TRANSITION FROM DISTINCT RINGS TO SPLAYED OUTLINE. *c.* 1300

possible to bring the apex of every arch composing it to the same level. The number of ribs is small; a cross rib, wall rib, and diagonal rib only being used. The diagonal rib is made semicircular, or nearly so,

FIG. 45. DIAPER
WESTMINSTER. *c.* 1250

FIG. 46
DOG-TOOTH ENRICHMENT

while the wall rib forms a sharply pointed arch.
This produces a twist in the spandrel-filling between
the two ribs, especially in oblong vaults, where the
difference between the diagonal and the shorter
side is considerable, and the twist is sometimes

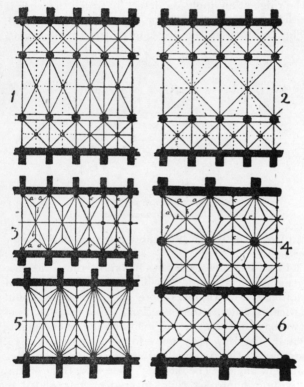

FIG. 47. PLANS OF VAULTS

1. Without and with ridge-ribs. 2. Sexpartite vault over nave. 3. Intermediate ribs (*a*) added; the ridge-rib (*b*) stopped against them, and (*c*)
continued beyond to the wall 4. The same. 5. More intermediate
ribs added. 6. Fourteenth-century lierne vault.

increased by stilting the shorter rib. This form of
vault has been aptly called ploughshare vaulting.
The courses in each division of the spandrel-filling
form approximately equal angles with the two ribs
on which they rest; consequently the courses meet
the ridge at an angle—a detail by which the work is
readily distinguished from that of a later period.
The keystone at the crossing of the two diagonals

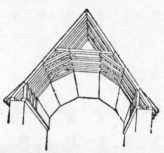

FIG. 48. TRUSSED-RAFTER ROOF
WITH AND WITHOUT CEILING

is often treated as a boss, and is carved with foliage
or figures.

In a large church the bays of the aisles are
generally nearly square, while the nave being about
double the width, has oblong bays, which are about
twice as wide as they are long. And so sometimes
two bays of the nave are included under one square
vault. In this case an additional groin is used,
similar to the diagonals, but crossing the building
at right angles. The bay has, therefore, three groins,
dividing it into six cells, instead of four, and it is,
therefore, called a sexpartite vault, the ordinary
plan being quadripartite. This kind is more commonly used in France than in England. Its æsthetic

effect is admirable, but it involves some constructional difficulties, and never became popular in
England.

Roofs are high-pitched. They belong to the class
known as 'trussed-rafter' roofs, that is, each pair
of rafters is framed together by a system of ties and

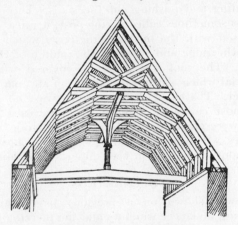

FIG. 49. TRUSSED-RAFTER ROOF
WITH RUDIMENTARY PRINCIPAL TRUSS

struts so as to be a complete truss in itself. In later
roofs the rafters were not so framed, but were
strengthened by purlins, carried on framed trusses,
or principals, placed at considerable intervals. The
two methods are, at this period, often combined in
a somewhat unscientific way, by using a rudimentary
principal in a trussed-rafter roof. There are no
principal rafters; the principal truss consists of a
very strong tie-beam, on the centre of which stands
a post cut into the form of a column, with capital
and base, supporting a central purlin. This purlin

helps to support the collars which stiffen the rafters. The purlin, therefore, gives but an indirect support to the rafter, and any weight which the tie-beam does carry comes upon the very middle of it. The heavy tie-beam is, however, of use in tying in the wall-plates, and thus preventing the rafters from spreading and pushing out the walls. The central post is sometimes called a king-post; it must not be confused with the modern king-post, which hangs from the ridge and supports the middle of the tie- · beam. The roof was generally covered with the material which was most available in any particular district. Thatch of straw or reeds was, no doubt, the most common; shingles would be used where oaks were plentiful, and thin slabs of stone, slates, or tiles where these could be obtained. Lead was commonly used only in very important buildings.

DECORATED

It was shown on a previous page how the grouping of lancet windows and the piercing of the space above them had produced plate-tracery. As the piercings become larger, narrow and irregular-shaped surfaces of stone are left between them. These are now themselves pierced, and thus the tracery lights are divided by bars of stone of the same thickness as the mullion. This development was reached rather before the middle of the thirteenth century. It has been called 'bar-tracery', a term which includes all the later forms as distinguished from plate-tracery.[1]

At first the heads of the principal lights have

[1] The English seem to have seldom used elaborate plate-tracery as they did on the Continent; when the piercings became numerous we wisely abandoned it for bar-tracery.

plain arches, while the circles in the
tracery are boldly cusped. But before
long the arches are cusped also. These
early cusps die into the level soffit of
the tracery and are called 'soffit-cusps';
but afterwards they are made wider,
and are moulded like the tracery.
Sometimes instead of being cusped the
whole tracery bar is foliated.[1]

FIG. 50
SIMPLEST BAR
TRACERY,
NORWICH.
c. 1240

This thirteenth-century tracery, consisting of simple forms, such as circles
and trefoils, is known as 'geometrical'. It is at this period that tracery
reaches its highest perfection of beauty and fitness.
Equal care is given to the shape of the piercing
and to the form of the bar. In the earlier plate
tracery attention had been confined to the shape of
the lights, and awkward masses of stone had been

FIG. 51. SOFFIT-CUSPING FIG. 52. ORDINARY CUSPING

left between. In later work, on the other hand, the
bending of the bar into graceful lines was all that
was thought of. The change appears at the beginning
of the fourteenth century. The heads of the lights
take the ogee form, the stonework follows sinuous
lines, and most of the piercings become irregular in
shape. It is then known as 'flowing tracery'.

Geometrical tracery, however, continues to be
used, though less often, till both sorts begin to give

[1] Fig. 58.

way to Perpendicular. The excessively florid work of France is called 'flamboyant'. We in England avoided this, but we descended to the dull monotony of 'reticulated' tracery,[1] in which one pattern is repeated all over the window-head. In the fourteenth century the form of the cusping changes.

FIG. 53. PERFECT TRACERY, THE TRIFORIUM, WESTMINSTER. *c.* 1250

The heads of the lights then have four small cusps instead of the two large cusps of the thirteenth century, and the tracery cusping corresponds.[2] Square-headed windows are not uncommon in churches, and are frequently used in domestic work. In this, as in the previous period, the transom was very rarely used, except when the lower part of the window was to open.

A remarkable change comes over the character of the carved foliage; an exact imitation of specific species was aimed at. The thirteenth-century sculptor had thrown into his work the life, the beauty, and the freedom of nature in the full vigour of growth, not troubling himself about any particular plant. His successor chose his plant and copied it as accurately as he could. This was a false step; but he went farther astray in taking as his ideal not the growing herbage, but a spray or wreath of leaves twisted round the capital as it might be for harvest

[1] Fig. 58.   [2] Fig. 56.

decorations; and in doing this he showed, too, that he did not appreciate the architectural value of the strong vertical stems of the Early English foliage. But it must be admitted that he copied his oak, vine, maple or what not, with extraordinary skill. Moreover, we must remember that his work was richly painted and gilded; his scheme was a colour scheme, heightened by modelling the surface. The colour is gone, and we have only the skeleton left.[1]

This change had taken place in France earlier than in England. At Westminster Abbey, where we might expect to find some French hands at work, there are a few capitals and a spandrel carved in this fashion. The treatment is perhaps generally more happy for a surface, such as a spandrel, than for a capital.

Columns are not very dissimilar to those of the preceding period; detached shafts of Purbeck marble are less frequently used.

The arch-mouldings become more elaborate and have numerous fillets on the rolls. They are not worked on the

[1] E. S. Prior.

FIG. 54. TRACERY WITH TWO VARIETIES OF CUSPING. CHOIR, LICHFIELD. c. 1300

5

face and soffit of each order as formerly, but on a
splayed surface; the distinction between the orders
had been gradually disappearing, and is finally lost
through the joint being concealed in a hollow. The

FIG. 55
FLOWING TRACERY

FIG. 56. SQUARE-HEADED
WINDOW, WITH TRACERY

FIG. 57. FLOWING TRACERY, GRANTCHESTER.
c. 1340

splayed surface has a wave-moulding or a sunk
chamfer. The hollows are fewer and shallower. They
disappear from the base towards the end of the
thirteenth century, and from the abacus and

FIG. 58. RETICULATED TRACERY MERTON COLLEGE, OXFORD.
c. 1310

FIG. 59
BALL-FLOWER
ENRICHMENT

FIG. 60
NATURAL FOLIAGE,
SOUTHWELL

hood-mould early in the fourteenth. The ball-flower is used instead of the dog-tooth, and often in too great profusion. The arch-mouldings of doors and windows are generally carried down the jamb instead of being stopped on a shaft.

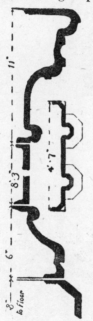

FIG. 61. MOULDED CAP AND BASE. *c.* 1320 WITH PLAN OF PIER REDUCED

FIG. 62. MOULDED BASE *c.* 1300

In diminutive work, such as niches and window tracery, the ogee arch is used, that is to say, the concave curve of the arch becomes convex near the point.

Several important changes occur in vaulting. In

order to reduce the size of the
spandrels, which in large vaults is
very considerable, additional ribs
(Fig. 47 *a a*) are introduced. Now a
pair of these intermediate ribs
form an arch, of which the two
sides lie in different planes. They
have therefore a tendency to fall
towards the centre of the vault.
In order to counteract this, a 'ridge
rib' (*b b*) is placed between the
apex of the intermediate pair of
ribs and the centre of the vault.
These ridge ribs are afterwards continued to the extremity of the
vault, but this continuation (*c c*) is
of no structural use. Another important alteration is that made in

FIG. 63
MOULDED CAPITAL
c. 1300

the curvature of the ribs. The curve of the diagonal
rib now approximates to the ellipse which would be
produced by the intersection of two cylindrical
spandrel surfaces of regular form. It is not, as a

matter of fact, actually an ellipse,
but an arch struck from several
centres. The courses of the spandrel-
filling are now made horizontal, so
that they are parallel with the ridge.
The ploughshare form of spandrel is
abandoned. About the middle of
the fourteenth century a further
modification is made by the introduction of 'lierne' ribs, that
is, ribs which do not spring from
the shaft or wall, but cross the
spandrels from rib to rib, producing

FIG. 64
MOULDED CAPITAL
c. 1320

star-shaped patterns. This variety is known as lierne vaulting.

As the walls are reduced in thickness and the

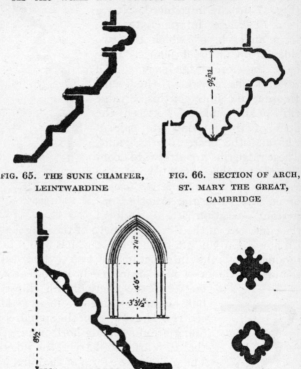

FIG. 65. THE SUNK CHAMFER, LEINTWARDINE

FIG. 66. SECTION OF ARCH, ST. MARY THE GREAT, CAMBRIDGE

FIG. 67. MOULDINGS ON THE SPLAYED FACE. 1350

FIG. 68. PLANS OF COLUMNS

thrusts of vaults and roofs increase and are more concentrated, the buttresses are given greater projection, and their depth begins to exceed their width. In the fourteenth century they are generally

FIG. 69. LIERNE VAULTING, ELY. *c.* 1330

FIG. 70
WEATHERING OF
BUTTRESS. 1350

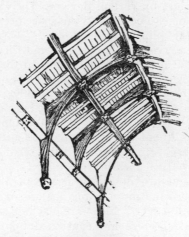

FIG. 71. ROOF WITH ARCHED PRINCIPALS
AND INTERMEDIATES, NORTH ELMHAM

placed diagonally at the corners of buildings, and they are more often terminated by gablets; the angles are not chamfered.

The trussed-rafter roof continues to be used, but roofs with purlins become more common. The principal truss has generally an arched form. A truss of this sort exerted a considerable thrust on the walls, but this was reduced as much as possible by carrying the arched struts a good distance down the wall. Where the principals are far apart, intermediate principals of a slightly different form are used, or the purlins are strengthened by wind-braces.

PERPENDICULAR

During the latter part of the fourteenth century and throughout the fifteenth, the extent of the wall surface is steadily reduced, actually and in appearance, by various devices. The windows are enlarged so as to occupy all the space between the buttresses; the plinth is heightened, so that there is little interval left between it and the sill of the window; the arches are made flat, so that the spandrels are reduced to insignificance. The parapet becomes an important and often a highly elaborate feature; it is generally battlemented, but no attempt was made to give it a really defensive appearance.

About the middle of the fourteenth century there begin to appear in the window tracery straight vertical members; at first they are generally short, and are not very noticeable.[1] But they quickly become more numerous and more pronounced, till all curved lines are excluded, and the mullions themselves are continued up to the arch. These vertical lines, of course, entirely alter the character

[1] Fig. 72.

of the tracery and of the whole building, so that the
term Perpendicular, as applied to the style, is
descriptive and appropriate. A transom, with sub-
arches, is used as an architectural feature, whereas
formerly it had been plain, and had been used only

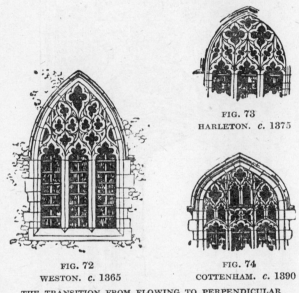

FIG. 73
HARLETON. *c.* 1375

FIG. 72
WESTON. *c.* 1365

FIG. 74
COTTENHAM. *c.* 1390

THE TRANSITION FROM FLOWING TO PERPENDICULAR
TRACERY

as a necessary division between the glazed upper
portion of the light and the shutter fitted in the
lower part. Short pieces of transom are also used in
the tracery itself. (Fig. 74.)

Large doorways are generally arched, but the
lintel is occasionally used. The most common
arrangement consists of an ordinary arch with two

FIG. 75

GATEWAY OF ST. JOHN'S COLLEGE, CAMBRIDGE. 1510

From 'Cambridge Described and Illustrated'

hood-moulds, one following the arch, the other being
horizontal, and turned down at each end to meet
the inner hood-mould at the springing of the arch.[1]
The spandrel included between the two hood-
moulds is filled with tracery, sculpture, or heraldry,
In small doorways the lintel is frequently used.
especially in domestic buildings, though it is often
given an arched form.[2] All or most of the mouldings
are carried down the jamb, often one member is
stopped on an extremely slender shaft. The hood-
mould is often of ogee form. (Fig. 75.)

The projection of the buttresses continues to
increase. The weatherings have a slightly wavy outline. The angles of the building sometimes have a
pair of buttresses, sometimes only one which is set
diagonally.

Columns are usually treated as a group of half-
shafts alternating with wide shallow hollows.[3] The
half-shafts alone have capitals and bases, the hollows
continuing up into coresponding hollows in the
arch, and at the bottom dying away in the plinth.
The arch being commonly blunt, the column
occupies a large proportion of the total height of an
arcade. The capitals are small proportionately to
the small shafts which they surmount; they are
seldom carved with foliage. The bases are of slight
projection, but are often mounted on a high plinth.

The arch has usually a blunt point, that is, the
two centres from which it is struck are close together.
But now a new form of arch appears, namely, one
struck from four centres. It springs with sharp
curves struck with a short radius from centres on
the level of the springing; the central part of the
arch is formed of arcs with a longer radius struck

[1] Fig. 77.   [2] Fig. 91.   [3] Fig. 78.

FIG. 76
WEST DOORWAY, CHESTER CATHEDRAL. *c.* 1490

from centres below the springing. The four-centred arch never entirely superseded the two-centred. It had long been used for the diagonal and intermediate ribs in vaulting, from which the idea was perhaps borrowed.

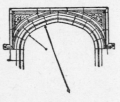

The mouldings of the arch are worked on a splayed face; they consist of a series of small members, such as ogees, separated from another similar group by a wide shallow hollow called a 'casement'; the soffit is narrow and flat; the hood-mould commonly has a straight,

FIG. 77

FOUR-CENTRED ARCH WITH DOUBLE HOOD-MOULD

sloping, upper surface, and an ogee or hollow below; the abacus of the capital is similar.

The foliage has deteriorated. It has neither the vigour and abstract beauty of the thirteenth-century carving, nor the imitative skill of the fourteenth century. It is hard and lifeless, and is used chiefly in the form of rosettes and similar ornaments.

Three enrichments are used: (1) leaves or flowers very conventionally treated, and varying in size according to the width of the hollow in which they

are placed, are used on jambs, arches, hood-moulds, capitals, string courses, and cornices; (2) battlements are an equally common form of ornament, and are used on the tops of capitals, cornices, and transoms; (3) a cresting of upright leaves or ' brattishing', of like

FIG. 78

PLAN OF PIER

character to those just mentioned, is used in the same positions as battlements.

Shallow sunk panels are now used as a system of decoration. They are applied at first to the plinth

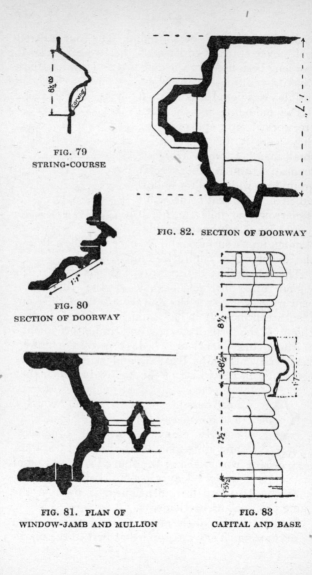

FIG. 79
STRING-COURSE

FIG. 82. SECTION OF DOORWAY

FIG. 80
SECTION OF DOORWAY

FIG. 81. PLAN OF
WINDOW-JAMB AND MULLION

FIG. 83
CAPITAL AND BASE

and to the battlements, then to the spandrels of
large arches and the faces of buttresses, and finally
in some late works the whole wall is covered. In
those districts where flint is obtainable, it is used in
combination with stone for external panelling; the

FIG. 84. FIGURE ON A
HAMMER-BEAM, CAWSTON

FIG. 85. ARCH-MOULD
WITH NICHES, SONNING

stone is cut to the required architectural forms to
represent the framework, and the flints are inserted,
their faces flush with the stone, to represent the
panels. The flints are split to show a smooth black
surface, and they are shaped with great nicety to
fit their positions.

Vaulting becomes more elaborate by the increase
in the number of ribs. The principal change, however, is in the curvature of the ribs. This change

produces a new variety of vault, known as 'fan-
vaulting', because the numerous ribs produce,
when seen from below, a somewhat fan-like appearance. All ribs have the same curve till they reach
the level of the apex of the shortest pair of ribs;
above this level the longer ribs are continued by a
very flat curve till they meet the ridge. Horizontal
ribs are used, though they are not, in fan-vaulting,
called lierne ribs; they form horizontal concentric

FIG. 86
BRATTISHING. 1538

circles, with their centre over the springing of the
vault, and hence they increase the resemblance to
a fan.[1]

The character of any vault is determined by
considering the form of the mass of masonry above
any one shaft. In the early vaults one of these
masses forms, roughly, an inverted half-pyramid
with concave sides, and a plan taken through it
gives a parallelogram. In fan-vaulting the bundle
of ribs forms an inverted half-cone of concave
section, and its plan is a semicircle. It is this
difference, more than any other—more even than
the network of ribs, tracery and carving with which
it is overlaid—that gives fan-vaulting its distinctive
character. The early vault has the effect of (and is,
as a matter of fact) a tunnel cut by cross-tunnels. In

[1] The old form of vault was till the end more common.

FIG. 87
FAN-VAULTING, TEWKESBURY. 1421

FIG. 88
PLAN OF FAN-VAULT, KING'S COLLEGE,
CAMBRIDGE. 1512

6

the fan-vault this character has, to its gain or loss, been eliminated both in fact and in appearance. The method of construction is also radically different. In the earlier vaults, the ribs were true arches— were, in fact, functional. They were built first,

FIG. 89. HAMMER-BEAM ROOF, COCHWILLAN

independently of the spandrels; the spandrels consisted of courses, each slightly arched, resting on the ribs. In the fan-vault the ribs and spandrels are one; the ribs are mere ornaments worked on the surface of the cone.

During the fourteenth century carpentry had been brought to great perfection. Roofs reach their highest development in that which is known as the 'hammer-beam roof'. In this construction a bracket, called the hammer-beam, rests on the top of the wall and projects into the building. This bracket supports a vertical post which stiffens the principal

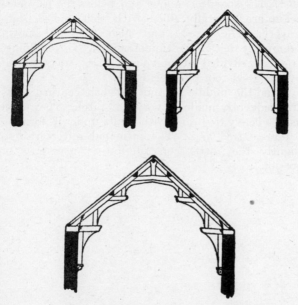

FIG. 90. DIAGRAMS OF HAMMER-BEAM ROOFS

rafter. The weight of this post is counteracted, partly by the weight of the principal rafter, which rests on the other end of the hammer-beam, and partly by a strut under it, springing from a corbel some way down the wall. The upper part of the principal is strengthened by a collar, or by another hammer-beam and post, or by curved struts, forming an arch with its apex quite close to the ridge.

This form of roof lends itself to many variations and to a highly decorative treatment. The hammer-beam is sometimes carved into the form of an angel, or an angel stands upon it in front of the vertical post. The spandrels above and below the hammer-beam are generally filled with rich and delicate tracery. The finest, and also the best-known example is that of Westminster Hall. This building, originally divided into nave and aisles, was spanned by one great roof by Richard II.

After the middle of the fifteenth century roofs are frequently made of very flat pitch. They then have a heavy tie-beam, with struts under it, forming a four-centred arch. The principal rafters rise so slightly that little construction is necessary or possible.

CHAPTER III
RENAISSANCE

TUDOR

AT the beginning of the sixteenth century Gothic architecture was practically dead. The little work that was done is, with some notable exceptions, it is true, poor in general design and meagre in detail. The windows have either hard and monotonous tracery or none at all, and the cusping is often omitted; roofs are flat and without architectural character; mouldings are shallow and give no contrasts of light and shade; carving has become hard and mechanical; vaults are masterpieces of ingenious masonry overloaded with detail. Everything was favourable therefore for the introduction of new ideas from abroad when the Reformation gave the *coup de grâce* to Gothic art.

But during the reign of Henry VIII the old traditions were carried on with little change. Here and there, especially in the south of England, Italian details are found mingled with the common English work, owing to the employment of Italian workmen. Wolsey's work at Hampton Court and Layer Marney House in Essex are well-known examples. The foreigner sometimes brought over terra-cotta

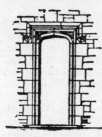

FIG. 91. DOORWAY,
WHITMINSTER.
c. 1500

panels or coloured marbles, or he carved, here, a band of arabesque ornament, or there, a classical cornice or a mantelpiece. But the main outline of the building continued to be pure Gothic, and where the builder was not too ambitious the result is charming. The wall with its plinth and parapet, its gable and buttresses, is very much what it was in the fifteenth century. Doorways generally have a lintel and a sub-arch, with heraldry carved in the spandrels. The windows are large, and consist of many lights under a very flat arch or a lintel. The heads of the lights have sub-arches, but they are uncusped. The oriel window in the hall of a large house becomes an important feature; lofty, richly vaulted, glowing with heraldic glass, it has a peculiar stateliness and beauty.

Early in the reign of Elizabeth the Italian workmen were succeeded by German and Flemish Protestants, who having fled from religious persecutions, settled in England and began to influence English architecture. Small buildings and those in remote country places were not very much affected;

but the palace of the nobleman, though built by
Englishmen, and more or less in the English manner,
was often finished off in the fashionable foreign
style. To what extent the wood and stone carvings
and the details of some of the masonry, the plaster-
work and the marble mantelpieces are the work of
foreigners is still under dispute. In some instances

FIG. 92
BASE OF A MONUMENT, SPILSBY. _c._ 1610

they show considerable power in design, but their
work is almost always overloaded with a profusion
of extremely bad ornament, and shows a lack of
judgment and restraint.

Indeed, at first the Renaissance makes but slow
progress. A cornice of classical profile finishes the
wall, but on this stands a parapet of Gothic form
or of open work of a peculiar character known as
strap-work.[1] The roof continues to be high-pitched.
The gable often has a curved outline—one of the
few Flemish fashions which took root in England.
Buttresses are now seldom used, but pilasters and

[1] Fig. 94.

columns have not yet taken their place. Chimneys, now almost always of brick, are very picturesquely treated; the flues are kept separate and grouped in various ways, or ornamented with spiral flutes, and surmounted with bold caps. In some of the more ambitious stone houses the chimneys are fashioned into the form of Roman columns.

It is chiefly on the doorway and porch that decoration is concentrated. The doorway has a round or

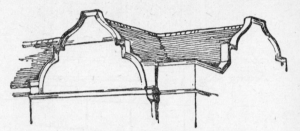

FIG. 93. CURVED GABLES, FEN DITTON

eliptical arch or a lintel, but in either case it is surrounded by a framework of Renaissance architecture—columns, entablature, and pediment. The windows do not alter in form. They are generally very simply treated, and are devoid of tracery; the great oriel of the hall has been generally discarded, but there are numerous small oriels. The moulding of the mullion, which has hitherto been concave, is now convex (Fig. 98).

The open timber roof is not very common, but in large halls the hammer-beam construction is still occasionally used, as in the hall of the Middle Temple, London, with Renaissance mouldings and other details. More generally the roof is hidden by a flat ceiling of rich plaster-work, the surface of which is divided into panels of varied shapes, containing devices, the broad bands which divide the panels being ornamented with a scroll of vine.

Oak panelling was extensively used, the panels being small and nearly square; the mouldings were worked partly on the edges of the stiles and rails, dying away as they approached the angle of the panel, and partly as grooves on the centre of the framing, those on the stiles being stopped abruptly by the rails which ran at right angles to them. The panels themselves are often worked with a peculiar series of mouldings, bearing some resemblance to a folded cloth, whence they are called linen-panels (Fig. 99).

In those parts of the building where Renaissance forms were adopted, the mouldings are of fairly correct classical profile; they will be described in a

FIG. 94. ORIEL WINDOW,
ST. JOHN'S COLLEGE, CAMBRIDGE. 1600

FIG. 95. CARVED BEAM, SHREWSBURY

FIG. 96. PLASTER CEILING,
ST. JOHN'S COLLEGE, CAMBRIDGE.
c. 1600

FIG. 97. ARABESQUE.
KING'S COLLEGE, CAMBRIDGE
c. 1535

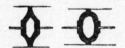

FIG. 98. MEDIEVAL AND
TUDOR MULLIONS

FIG. 99. LINEN-PANEL AND
TUDOR FRAMING

later section (p. 69). But the English workman still
continued to use the traditional Perpendicular
mouldings in a somewhat debased form in the less
important parts of the building.

The timber buildings of this period are picturesque and often richly ornamented with a coarse but effective mixture of Gothic and Renaissance detail. The traditional methods of construction with overhanging upper storeys continue in use. The bargeboards which finish the gables are decorated with pierced tracery or are carved in relief.

The sixteenth century was a period of transition from the dead Gothic to the architecture of the Renaissance, which was to be introduced from the Continent in the following century. It was also an age of transition from the medieval system (in which the design had been worked out on the spot, and the details had been entrusted to the inherited knowledge of the craftsman[1]) to the modern method of getting a design from an architect at a distance who draws every detail and exercises a supreme control over the whole work. In this interval between the death of the old traditional style and the appearance of the first architect, building was done in a somewhat haphazard way. New features were grafted on to the old stock in an arbitrary and clumsy manner, by men who were often ignorant of their proper purpose.

STUART

The trained artist who was to introduce the new style and to inaugurate the new system, appeared early in the reign of James I. Inigo Jones had been born in 1573. He had studied architecture in Italy, especially the works of Palladio, and on his return to England had spent some ten years in miscellaneous occupations and in designing scenes for the elaborate masques then in vogue among the nobility. In 1619

[1] In the less important buildings.

he made plans for the new royal palace of Whitehall. The execution of this immense scheme, consisting of three great courts, was delayed by the financial difficulties of the King, and was finally stopped by the outbreak of the Civil War. The beautiful Banqueting House, the only part of the plan which was ever carried out, was almost the first work of Inigo Jones. It may be said to have revolutionized English architecture. It was the first building which entirely discarded the dying Gothic tradition and frankly accepted the new style which had been but slowly making its way for the last hundred years. It was the first building in which one hand, and one only, is to be seen from beginning to end. But though Inigo Jones may be said to have introduced into England the style of the Italian architects, of whom Palladio is in this country commonly taken as the representatives, it became in his hands an English style. The Banqueting House, although the first building of its kind in England, and the work of a man who had learned his art in Italy, is yet thoroughly English in character.

The classical Orders now for the first time become an integral part of the building; they are employed with more complete knowledge, and with an understanding of their proper use. This will, therefore, be an appropriate place to give some account of them (Figs. 103–5).

By an Order is meant the column and its superstructure. It includes (1) a plinth or podium, consisting generally of a series of steps, but sometimes of a high pedestal with a base and capping; (2) the column, including the base, shaft, and capital; (3) the entablature, which consists of three parts, namely, the architrave, forming a lintel immediately

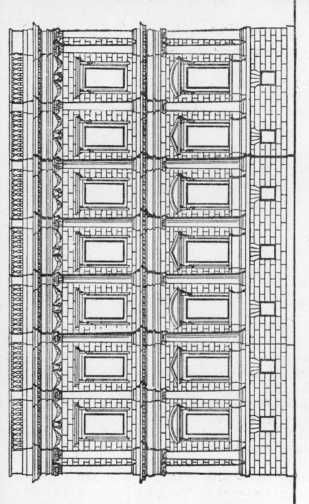

FIG. 100. THE BANQUETING HOUSE, WHITEHALL PALACE
By INIGO JONES, 1619. *From 'Vitruvius Britannicus'*

above the capital, the frieze or broad band frequently decorated, and the cornice or boldly projecting top member.

The Orders are five in number. Three of them—the Doric, Ionic, and Corinthian—were used and perfected by the Greeks. The Romans modified these, and produced two others of less importance,

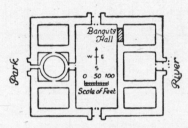

FIG. 101. BLOCK PLAN OF WHITEHALL PALACE
From 'Later Renaissance Architecture in England'

namely, the Tuscan and Composite. The five Roman Orders were revived by the Italian architects of the fifteenth century, and their employment was reduced to rigid rules of proportion. Although the proportions fixed by these rules were not strictly adhered to by the ancients, it must be understood that their invention and employment was not so absurd in the case of the classical style as it would be in others, such as Gothic. Even in the absence of rules, the size of the various parts of a classical building maintained, roughly, a constant ratio to the whole, while their number was always the same, whatever the size of the building. Thus the diameter of a Greek Doric column is always about two-elevenths of the height, whether that be ten feet or forty. And so with the mouldings and with every detail. The half-diameter of the column is taken as the standard, and is called a module. In the Gothic style the size of the parts remains nearly constant in large buildings and small, and their number varies.

FIG. 102. LINDSAY HOUSE, LONDON
By INIGO JONES, c. 1625. *From 'Vitruvius Britannicus'*

The Greek Doric has a massive column divided into twenty flutes; it is without a base, and has a very simple capital, with a square abacus. The architrave is plain, and the frieze is divided into triglyphs and metopes. The triglyph consists of three projecting vertical fillets. They are supposed to be derived from the ends of the beams which were visible in the early timber buildings. The metopes are square spaces between the triglyphs, and are filled with sculpture. The Romans spoilt this order by making the column more slender and by omitting the flutes and elaborating the simple Greek capital; they made the architrave shallower and omitted the sculpture in the metopes. The Italian architects of the Renaissance fluted the shaft and added a base. The Greek Doric had no enrichments; the Romans and Italians used dentils in the cornice.

The Ionic Order is slender in its proportions. The column has a base, and the capital is ornamented with volutes or spirals, which are the most characteristic feature of the order. The shaft is fluted with twenty-four flutes, which are separated by flat fillets. The entablature is light compared with the Doric entablature, and the frieze is plain. Dentils and the egg-and-dart are used. The Romans did not modify this order greatly. The Italians copied the Roman order but introduced a great deal of sculpture into the entablature.

The Corinthian Order resembles the Ionic in its general proportions. Like the Ionic, its distinguishing feature is its capital, which is ornamented with rows of acanthus leaves and with small volutes at the angles. The mouldings are enriched with various leaf ornaments. This rich order was the favourite of the Romans, and they were more successful with it than with any other. They treated the acanthus in a more luxuriant manner than the Greeks, and enriched the frieze and many of the mouldings of the entablature with sculpture.

The Romans occasionally used a variation of the Roman Doric, which they called Tuscan. They also invented a Composite Order, in which the

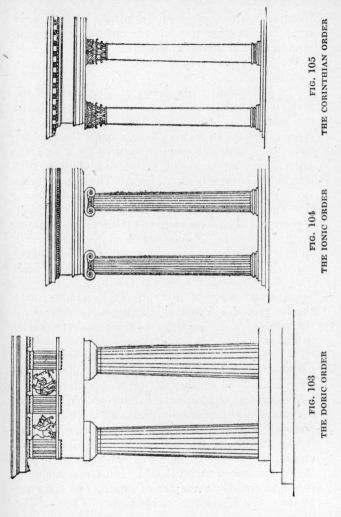

FIG. 103

THE DORIC ORDER

FIG. 104

THE IONIC ORDER

FIG. 105

THE CORINTHIAN ORDER

features of the Ionic and Corinthian capitals were combined; in other respects the order bore a general resemblance to the Corinthian.

We may now return to our view of modern architecture.

The Renaissance architects, of course, copied the Roman, not the Greek varieties. They also observed the same rules when using several orders in the same building. In Roman and in early Renaissance times each storey is usually marked by a separate order. In that case the simplest and most substantial is always placed lowest. Thus, in a three-storeyed building, the lowest order would be Doric, the next Ionic, and the uppermost Corinthian. Sometimes the lowest storey is treated as a podium, and is 'rusticated' in one way or another to give it a substantial appearance. Two storeys, but never more than two, are sometimes included in one order. This is occasionally done in the first half of the seventeenth century, and almost invariably after the Restoration. When a building has four storeys, the uppermost is placed above the main cornice and is treated as a small separate order, called an Attic Order—hence our use of this classical word for a garret—the two middle floors are included in the main order, and the lowest forms a podium.

The system of moulding in classical architecture is essentially different from that of the Gothic style. Medieval architecture was a system of arches, and it was the arch which was emphasized by elaborate mouldings. A true cornice was seldom used, and to the end remained undeveloped. But Greek architecture was entirely a matter of lintels, and the style retained this character without much change. The proportions and decoration of the entablature had been settled approximately in remote times; the latter by the timber construction of the earliest buildings. The plain Doric architrave is the lintel, the triglyphs represent the ends of the beams of the roof, the cornice is the overhanging eaves. Though variations were made in details, the general arrangement, illustrating its structural origin, was preserved and perfected in the unchanging East, and has never been seriously modified. The Romans did use the arch for structural purposes, but architecturally they always kept it subordinate to the entablature. Its face was ornamented with a repetition of the very simple architrave moulding, and the soffit was plain. This restraint was necessary on æsthetic grounds. The elaboration and emphasis of a richly moulded arch under the string lines and deep shadow of the entablature would be an artistic blunder.

Mouldings do not vary as much as in Gothic architecture. They are grouped in each order according to recognized rules. Like other details in the classical styles, they are enlarged or reduced so as to maintain a fixed ratio to the height of the column. The number of enrichments varies according to circumstances. Other forms of decoration, such as festoons of flowers, were also copied from the Roman—a guide to be followed warily in matters of art; draperies and the skulls of oxen have even less in their favour than 'swags' as forms of decoration.

Where arches are used they spring from pilasters between the main columns.[1] They are invariably round, and generally have a projecting keystone,

[1] Inside a building an arch may spring from the entablature of the main order.

either plain or shaped to form a corbel to support the entablature. The 'flat-arch', as it is called, which had been occasionally used in the Middle Ages, now becomes common.

For purposes of vaulting an area is always divided into squares. Each of these is covered with a quadripartite vault formed by four round barrel

a   b

FIG. 106. CHIMNEY STACK,
CLARE COLLEGE,
CAMBRIDGE

FIG. 107. *a*, ARCH WITH
STEPPED EXTRADOS;
b, RUSTICATED QUOINS

vaults like those of the Romans and early Normans. The groins formed by the intersections of these vaults have no ribs.

The windows are high and narrow, without mullions or transoms, and in strong contrast with the windows, many-mullioned, wide and low, of the Elizabethan age. They are sometimes arched, but usually square-headed. The head and jambs have the common architrave mouldings, and there is sometimes also a complete entablature, with or without a pediment, over the head; the sill projects beyond the face of the wall, which was never the case in Gothic work; and the glass is fixed in a wood frame. In rusticated work the window has generally either a round or flat arch, and is quite plain. Large windows of three lights divided by columns are used; the side lights are narrow and covered by an entablature, the centre light is wide and arched. These are called Venetian windows. Doorways are made to correspond with the windows.

The ceilings are sometimes enriched with plaster work in relief and sometimes with paintings. In the former case the treatment is quite different from

SCALE 0 5 10 FEET

FIG. 108. PLAN OF CEILING
LIBRARY OF PEMBROKE COLLEGE, CAMBRIDGE. 1690

that of the preceding age. Instead of an intricate network of small panels, there is a central device with scrollwork disposed round it. Sometimes we have heavy beams covered with enriched mouldings of plaster dividing the space up into a few large, deeply recessed hollows or coffers, the central space being often filled with an oval or a circle.

The framework of the roof is never allowed to show. It is almost always hipped, so that there are no gables except where a pediment is required for architectural effect. In the latter part of the seventeenth century a new form of roof was introduced called a 'Mansard roof', after the French architect of that name. In order to obtain more space in the garrets, the lower part of the roof was made steep and the upper part nearly flat. This was the result of a change in the normal plan from a long narrow range to a square block. When there were no garrets the whole roof was usually of a rather low pitch and was hidden by a balustrade above the cornice. In the simpler buildings, however, especially in the country, steep roofs with gables continued to be

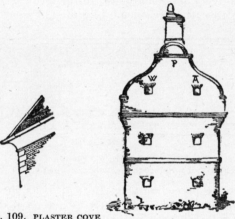

FIG. 109. PLASTER COVE
UNDER EAVES. 1670   FIG. 110. CURVED GABLE

used, and the balustrade is often omitted, the eaves projecting over a cornice or a plaster cove. The gables were often curved, but the curves were generally large ogees instead of the succession of small quadrants used in Elizabethan times.

The panelling of the humbler buildings, where the old traditions were followed, continued to be in small divisions with minute mouldings. But in the more correctly classical buildings the work was on a bolder scale and more in harmony with the style. The panels were very large and the edges were bevelled; they were surrounded by 'bolection' mouldings, that is, with mouldings projecting beyond the face of the framework. The mouldings also were 'mitred', that is, they were cut so as to intersect at the angles like an ordinary picture-frame.

It is necessary to notice here the long survival of the Gothic tradition contemporaneously with the practice of pure Palladian architecture. In some localities, as Oxford for instance, and in church work in general, the old forms lingered on, though mixed with classical details. Indeed there was in some sort a revival of the Gothic style in church building along with the renewed sense of decency and order which Archbishop Laud brought about. Few entire churches were built at this

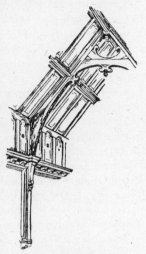

FIG. 111
JACOBEAN GOTHIC ROOF,
WHITWELL. *c.* 1635

time, the old buildings being in most places enough, and more than enough, for the wants of the congregation; Saint John's Church at Leeds is one of the few exceptions. It is usually in pulpits and other furniture, and occasionally in a new roof, that the movement is seen. In places where the old tradition was strong, such as the University towns, the old style had continued with little change. The buildings of Clare College, Cambridge, are an illustration.[1] The library of St. John's College is an

[1] They were robbed of some of their medieval features in the eighteenth century.

example of the revived Gothic. Though built in
1623, it has, combined with its classical cornices,
windows filled with Decorated tracery.

There was little building of any kind in England
between 1640 and 1660. The outbreak of the Civil
War necessarily put a stop to the practice of the
arts, and little work was done during the Commonwealth. But with the Restoration there was a
return of activity, and six years later the Fire of
London gave an opportunity such as has seldom
occurred. Christopher Wren was then thirty-four
years old. He had already made a reputation as a
mathematician, and had been appointed Professor
of Astronomy at Oxford. He had built the Chapel of
Pembroke College, Cambridge, for his uncle, Matthew
Wren, Bishop of Ely, and had begun the Sheldonian
Theatre at Oxford, besides other buildings. He
had studied for six months in Paris, then the best
school of architecture in Europe, and had been consulted about alterations to old Saint Paul's Cathedral.

Wren's first task after the Fire was the prepara-
tion of a general plan for laying out the whole city
except the extreme north-east portion. A wide em-
banked quay along the river, and an orderly arrangement of parallel streets, with main thoroughfares
sixty feet wide, converging on the most important
sites, were the chief features of this admirable
plan. The scheme was approved by the King, but
considerations of expense and private interests
prevented its execution.

Wren, who was now Surveyor-General, was
immediately consulted about St. Paul's Cathedral.
Several designs which he made for this were rejected,
and it was not till 1675 that the first stone was
laid. The building was opened for service on 2nd

December, 1697, and the lantern of the dome finished in 1710; but it was not till about ten years later that the whole work was actually complete. The cost was about £730,750, exclusive of sums spent on attempts to repair the old building. During the delays in beginning the cathedral, Wren was gaining experience in rebuilding the City churches. These churches, which numbered fifty-three, show an

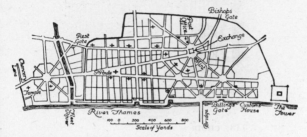

FIG. 112. WREN'S PLAN FOR REBUILDING THE CITY
From 'English Renaissance Architecture'

extraordinary variety of treatment and the most striking ingenuity in dealing with cramped and irregular sites. Besides these Wren designed Greenwich Hospital, Chelsea Hospital, Hampton Court, the Library of Trinity College, Cambridge, and other buildings. He died in 1723.

The grandeur of Wren's genius is patent. His strength lay in the largeness of his general conceptions; of the laborious perfecting of every detail he was inclined to be somewhat careless. One of his most striking qualities is the extraordinary ingenuity he displayed in the solution of a difficulty, whether æsthetic or constructional. He must be ranked below Inigo Jones as an artist. His manner is much less severe; indeed, his contemporaries and successors affected to be shocked at his freedom. But though his immediate following among the pedants of the next generation was consequently not so great as it

FIG. 113.   CHOIR SCHOOL, SALISBURY.   *c.* 1700

might have been, his influence on the architecture of the country generally was immense, and his style became, in fact, the national style.

HANOVERIAN

Before the close of the seventeenth century there had begun a reaction against Wren's free style in favour of a more correct imitation of Palladio. Chatsworth, by Talman, 1681, may be taken as an example. The charming little Exchange (now the Customs House) at King's Lynn, built in the same year, is typical of the school that was passing away (Fig. 114).

Early in the eighteenth century a diversion was created by the appearance of the amateur, a product highly characteristic of the age. There followed a succession of pedanic dilettanti, who, although not

entirely separable from the professional architects,
with whom indeed they generally worked, may be
considered as a distinct and not very healthy
influence. They may be connected to the main
stream of architecture by Hawksmoor and Vanbrugh. Nicholas Hawksmoor, although a pupil and
for many years an assistant of Wren's, fell under
the influence of Vanbrugh, with whom he worked,
assisting him with his professional knowledge.[1]
John Vanbrugh, the most famous of the amateurs,
took up architecture comparatively late in life.
Castle Howard, 1702, and Blenheim, 1705, are
characteristic products of an eccentric without
restraint, but not altogether without genius.
'Ponderous' perhaps best describes the characteristic for which his buildings are almost proverbial.
Henry Aldrich, Dean of Christ Church, built All
Saints' Church, Oxford; and Sir James Borough, the
master of Gonville and Caius College, was, at least
nominally, the architect of Clare College Chapel.
But, in truth, each of these gentlemen had to divide
the honours with a shadowy architect, who always
appears dimly in the background. This division of
fame is especially difficult in the case of the celebrated Earl of Burlington (1695–1753), who has by
some been placed little below Inigo Jones, while by
others he is, perhaps, with greater justice regarded
as little more than a particularly enlightened
patron. In connexion with this wave of amateurism
may be mentioned the perpetration, by professional
architects at the instance of their patrons, of such
absurdities as the reproduction of Italian villas,
as at Mereworth Castle and Foot's Cray, with every
circumstance which could make them inconvenient.

[1] Blomfield.

ORIGINALLY
OPEN

ORIGINALLY
OPEN

0 1 2 3 4 5 6 7 8 9 10 FEET
SCALE

FIG. 114. CUSTOMS HOUSE, KING'S LYNN
By BELL. 1681. *From a drawing by Mr. C. O. King*

The succession of practical architects begins again with the name of James Gibbs (1682–1754). After studying on the Continent he built the church of St. Mary-le-Strand (1714–17), in which Wren's influence is seen, and completed the steeple of Wren's church of St. Clement Danes. His best work

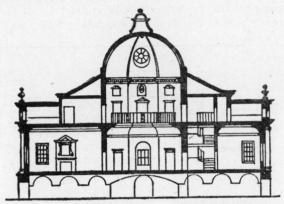

FIG. 115. SECTION OF ITALIAN VILLA
FOOT'S CRAY PLACE, KENT. *c.* 1720
From 'Vitruvius Britannicus'

is his church of St. Martin-in-the-Fields, with its noble portico (1721–6); in this, and in all his later works, he drops the florid style of St. Mary-le-Strand. He also built the Senate House and the Fellows' Buildings at King's College, Cambridge, and, in his later years, the Radcliff Library at Oxford, besides many other buildings.

Somewhat senior to Gibbs, but belonging to a later school, was Colin Campbell, the author of *Vitruvius Britannicus*. He built Mereworth, Kent, and Houghton, in Norfolk, which was finished and altered by Ripley. Ripley also designed, about 1726,

the Admiralty Offices, a building somewhat antici-
pating the gloomy manner of the next generation,
when Robert Adam added the gateway and screen.
The Horse Guards, a fine building, was designed, in
1742, by Kent, who also built Devonshire House
(portico added since), and Holkham, in Norfolk.
Among several provincial architects worthy of note
may be mentioned the Woods, father and son, of

FIG. 116. WENTWORTH HOUSE
By FLITCROFT. 1740. *From Jones's 'Views'*

Bath. Many of the buildings and the admirable
laying out of some parts of the city are due to them,[1]
and their house of Prior Park, near Bath, is a
remarkably stately and beautiful building.

The second half of the century began to show
that tendency towards a combination of the finicking
and the dull, which was to culminate in the work
of the brothers Adam. But Kedleston Hall, Derby,
and Thorndon Hall, Essex, by Paine, and Harewood
House, Yorkshire, by Carr, another provincial
architect of ability, are bold designs. The front of
the University Library at Cambridge is a pretty
piece of work by Wright.[2]

Sir William Chambers made a strong but un-
successful protest against the tendency of the age

[1] Blomfield.   [2] Fig. 120.

by his powerful designs for Somerset House and
many other buildings. His pupil, Gandon, followed
in his steps in his Dublin Customs House. George
Dance, the younger, who built St. Luke's Hospital,
Old Street, and Newgate Prison, has been called the
last of the old school.

It is in the deterioration of the general design

FIG. 117. HEAD OF DOORWAY,
OSWESTRY

FIG. 118. LEAD RAIN-
WATER HEAD, CHESTER

rather than in the use of new forms in the details
that the changes of the eighteenth century are most
clearly seen. A technical change in the method of
laying bricks at the end of the seventeenth century
may be noted as a useful guide to the date of a
building: English bond, which had hitherto been
employed, now gave place to Flemish bond. Arches
with stepped extrados (Fig. 117) are used more
frequently as time goes on.

The most striking architectural production of the
eighteenth century was the grand and somewhat
incongruous country house. An almost essential
feature is the great central portico, of one order,

equal to the whole height of the house. The smaller
houses, of less ambitious design and the work of

FIG. 119. GATEWAY OF ST. CATHERINE'S COLLEGE,
CAMBRIDGE, 1679
From 'Cambridge Described and Illustrated'

unknown men, often have the great merit of appropriateness to their purpose and to their surroundings,

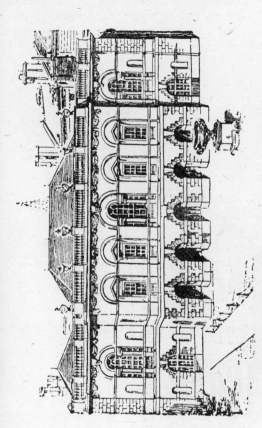

FIG. 120. FRONT OF THE UNIVERSITY LIBRARY, CAMBRIDGE
By WRIGHT. 1755. *From 'Cambridge Described and Illustrated'*

and the charm of modesty and repose. Every country town still retains a few street houses of this period; the walls of deep red or warm, dark brown brick, with bright red dressings and cornice, and rows of heavy sash windows, their rooms panelled and their mantelpieces of handsome marbles.

FIG. 121. HOUSE IN BURY ST. EDMUNDS

CHAPTER IV
CHURCHES

THE English church is the result of a gradual and steady development from the earliest times. It is a national product, resulting from the combination of two imported types, generally known as the Basilican and the Celtic. It will be necessary to give some account of these before describing their introduction into England and their effect on English architecture.

The Basilican arrangement varies in some important respects in different examples, but the normal plan may be thus described. The building consists of a nave,[1] with one or sometimes two aisles on each side, with galleries, called *triforia*, above them. It is entered from the east, as will presently be described. At the west end of the nave

[1] Figs. 123, 124.

there is a semicircular apse forming the presbytery, with a stone bench for the clergy round it, the middle seat being a raised chair for the bishop. In front of the bishop's chair, and nearly on the chord of the apse, is the altar. The western part of the nave is enclosed by screens (*cancelli*, whence our word 'chancel'), and forms a quire for the singers. The presbytery, and perhaps the quire, are raised considerably above the nave over a crypt called a

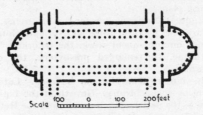

FIG. 122. PLAN OF A PAGAN BASILICA
From Middleton's 'Remains of Ancient Rome'

confessio,[1] the burial-place of saints. There are two staircases leading down from the church to the *confessio*, and if the vault of the *confessio* is sufficiently raised to allow of it there is a window in the wall between the *confessio* and the nave. There are sometimes transepts; in some cases these are as long as the nave, while in others they hardly project beyond the aisles. The church is entered by three doors through a *narthex*, or large porch, extending across the east end. On this side of the church, there is a fore-court surrounded by a cloister, and with a laver in the middle. Occasionally the entrances to the church are at the sides, and there is an apse at the east end as well as at the west.

[1] Fig. 126.

The development of this plan in its main outlines may be traced back to several sources, but the exact degree to which it was influenced by each of these is still a matter of dispute. It used to be held that the Basilican church was modelled directly on the pagan basilicas of Rome, or even that these were appropriated by Christians and converted into churches. But that could scarcely have been the process. During the greater part of the first three centuries the Christian communities met where opportunity offered: in private houses, at the alcoves erected over the burial-places of martyrs, and probably in *scholae* similar to those used by the numerous pagan fraternities, with which the Christian congregations had some practices in common.[1] In all buildings of that period the apse was the commonest of architectural features. For a building of any kind in which people were to assemble for a common object and with concentrated attention, an oblong room with an apse at one end was the most convenient and the most obvious plan, and it is accordingly an arrangement which is to be found in Roman buildings of every class. The public basilicas were primarily exchanges and secondarily law-courts.[2] They were of various forms, and some of them had apses with seats round, and an altar in the centre of the apse, and a *triforium* or gallery over the aisles. But the early Christians, even when fully tolerated, could hardly have held their meetings in busy and noisy exchanges. For more than two and a half centuries, therefore, they had been accustomed to meet in other buildings, and they must surely in that time

---

[1] Professor Baldwin Brown.
[2] The reason why these buildings were called basilicas, meaning 'royal,' is obscure.

have developed fully a normal arrangement for their buildings, or at least for the most important part, namely, the presbytery.

When at the end of the third century and in the time of Constantine the increased number of converts made more accommodation necessary, the simplest way of providing it was by a building with nave and

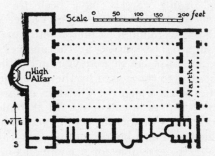

FIG. 123. OLD BASILICA OF ST. PETER, ROME
From Scott's 'English Church Architecture'

aisles, with a gallery over the aisles and with a clearstory, like the secular basilicas and other pagan buildings. The apse with its seats and altar had, without doubt, long since become stereotyped. The cloistered forecourt had always been familiar in the *atrium* of the private house. The alcove or cella erected in the cemetery outside the town over the tomb of the saint was rebuilt as a *confessio*, when the great numbers who visited the spot made it necessary to provide a large church. The end of the church at which the apse was placed was sometimes enlarged by the addition of transepts, thus forming a T-shaped plan, from which the cruciform plan was afterwards developed; thus in this, as in so many

other instances, a symbolical meaning was attached
to what was at first purely practical and utilitarian.
The term basilica had been applied to the great
halls of palaces as well as to exchanges, and it was
appropriated to the typical church plan early in the
fourth century. The features which the two had in
common, namely, the aisles with the galleries over

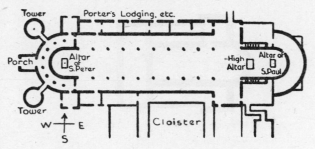

FIG. 124. CHURCH OF BASILICA TYPE, ST. GALL
From Scott's 'English Church Architecture'

them, the apse and the clearstory, are sufficiently
obvious to make the term perfectly appropriate.

The Basilican church plan was introduced into
England by the Romans. A good example of a small
church is that at Silchester, though unfortunately
only the foundations and part of the pavement
remain. It consists of a nave with an apse at the
west end, aisles, transepts, and a narthex or portico.
The foundation-walls between the nave and aisles
doubtless supported a row of columns, but one at
least of the transepts appears to have been separated
by walls from the rest of the church; the narthex
probably was an open portico with three doorways
leading into the church. The pavement is a mosaic
of *tessarae* made of red tiles cut into one-inch squares

in the manner common in Roman work. In the middle of the apse, however, there is a square with a pattern of black, white, and red *tesserae*; this marks the position of the altar, and shows also that it was of wood, as were also the seats round the apse. To the east of the church there was a laver, at which worshippers washed before entering, and near it

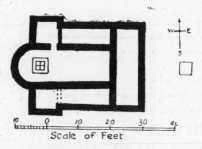

FIG. 125. ROMANO-BRITISH CHURCH, SILCHESTER
From 'Archæologia'

was a well. There were no distinct remains of the *atrium*, which, it has been suggested, surrounded the church instead of lying to the east of it as was usual.[1]

On the arrival of St. Augustine in 598, he found the church of St. Martin at Canterbury in use by Queen Bertha, the Christian wife of King Ethelbert. The nave of this church is still standing and forms the chancel of the present building.[2] Of St. Augustine's cathedral church no fragment is now to be seen. A description of it as it appeared in the middle of the eleventh century is preserved by Eadmer, though how much of the building then standing was the work of St. Augustine we cannot now say. It then had an apse at each end, with an altar slightly

[1] W. H. St. John Hope.   [2] J. T. Micklethwaite.

in advance of the chord of the apse; at the extreme
west end was the bishop's throne. The eastern altar
was in Eadmer's time considered the high altar, the
confessio was beneath it, and the choir of singers was
at the east end of the nave and was enclosed by a
screen.

The question of the orientation of churches is far
too large to enter upon here. Suffice it to say that
an entrance facing the rising sun is an arrangement
which the earlier Christian churches share with
buildings so various and so distant as the Parthenon,
the Temple of Jerusalem, and Stonehenge. The sub-
sequent turning round of the church is involved in
obscurity. It has been suggested by more than one
writer[1] that churches with two apses were fairly
common, and that the western apse, which had
originally contained the high altar, was gradually
superseded in importance by the east apse, and its
altar finally moved to the east part of the nave.
Others hold that the altar at the east end was always
the more common arrangement everywhere.[2] It
had never, it would seem, been held to be very
important which way the building or the congregation faced, if the priest faced east. The early
churches of Rome have the altar to the west, copying Antioch—the earliest centre of the Church—with
western altar carrying on the tradition of the pagan
temples. But places evangelized from Ephesus, which
succeeded Antioch in the supremacy, would have the
eastern altar, for there the temple of Diana and the
churches had the eastern altar.[3]

[1] G. G. Scott, jun., and J. T. Micklethwaite.
[2] H. E. Savage, *Proc. Soc. Antiq.*, *Newcastle-upon-Tyne*,
viii, 21.
[3] Church Quarterly Review, vol. CXXVIII, No. 256, July–
September 1939,

Other English churches of St. Augustine's time have one apse, and that to the east. Several have a *confessio*, varied in detail in the different examples,

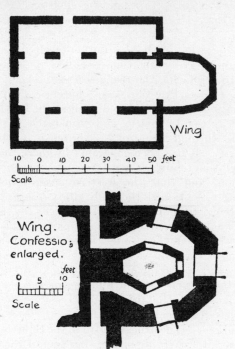

FIG. 126. THE BASILICA PLAN, WING
From the 'Archæological Journal'

but all with the same general plan of a central chamber with a passage round three sides, from which *arcisolia*, that is to say, recesses or chambers for other tombs, project.[1] There was a small square

[1] Wing, Fig. 126.

western porch, which was entered apparently from
a cloister abutting on it to the north and south;
to the west of the porch there was a baptistery.[1]
Some of these early churches have three arches
between the nave and the presbytery, possibly
because the builders lacked either the skill or the
courage to turn one large arch.[2]

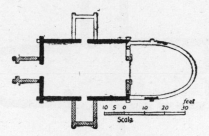

FIG. 127. TRANSITIONAL PLAN,
ST. PANCRAS, CANTERBURY
From the 'Archæological Journal'

The cruciform plan was, it would seem, developed
in England more or less independently of, though
no doubt it was influenced by, the Continental
development. The north and south porches were
not porches only, but also contained altars. In St.
Augustine's Church at Canterbury the south porch
was also used as a supreme court of law, in which
were heard cases which could not be tried elsewhere
and the court itself became known as the *Suthdure*.[3]
These projecting wings, it had been argued, were
then moved farther east and their outer doors

[1] Indications of this at Brixworth, Northants.
[2] St. Pancras, Canterbury (Fig. 127). C. E. Peers, *Archæ.
Jour.*, lviii.
[3] G. G. Scott, jun.

omitted,[1] thus forming transepts with very small arches towards the nave.[2]

Something must now be said about that other influence on English church architecture, namely, the Celtic tradition. This is indeed the more important of the two, though its story is sooner told.

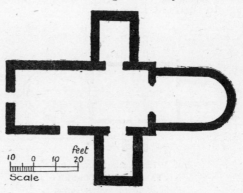

FIG. 128. TRANSITIONAL PLAN, WORTH
From the 'Archæological Journal'

A comparison of the Saxon churches of the North, built under the influence of the Irish missionaries, with the early Christian buildings of Ireland reveals some striking similarities; between these and the Basilican churches of the South there are equally obvious contrasts. The Irish Church had worked out for itself a simple, but quite definite, system of architecture. Its buildings were a development, it would appear, of the pagan cell or tomb, circular in plan, and in section of the form known as 'beehive', that is, with a stone roof made by corbelling out

[1] St. Pancras at Canterbury (above), and Worth (Fig. 128), illustrate two stages in the process.
[2] J. T. Micklethwaite.

every course beyond the one below it till the opposite
sides met at the top. This cell the Christians gradually
made square in plan. Sometimes there is an oblong
sanctuary at the east end; this
perhaps originated in a rectangular recess for the altar.
The towers are narrow and
lofty.[1]

St. Aidan and his fellow-
missionaries arrived in North-
umbria from St. Columba's
Irish settlement in Iona in
635, and were established at
Lindisfarne. They naturally
continued to build in the style
to which they had been accustomed,[2] and the tradition
was carried on by the great
building abbot Benedic Biscop
(628?–690), and to some extent perhaps by St. Wilfrid
(634–709), notwithstanding his
strong preference for Roman
to Columban ways. Their
churches are small and aisleless, and have a square-ended
chancel opening into the nave
by a narrow archway; there
are side porches and a western
tower.

FIG. 129. TOWER OF
MONKWEARMOUTH CHURCH
A.D. 674
*Drawn by Professor Baldwin
Brown*

This northern influence was felt far more widely
and rapidly than that of the Roman mission at
Canterbury, which seems to have been confined to
the extreme south-east. When the two met and

[1] Monkwearmouth (Fig. 129).   [2] Escomb (Fig. 130).

united, in the second half of the seventh century, a
type of building was evolved which was something
of a compromise between the Basilican and Celtic
plans, with a balance in favour of the latter. The
choir becomes a distinct chamber instead of a mere
enclosure of screens in the eastern part of the nave;
the apse is abandoned for the square presbytery;
the tall west tower is adopted; the transepts are
developed; side entrances are preferred to one at

Scale: 1 in. = 42 ft.

FIG. 130. CELTIC PLAN, ESCOMBE

From the 'Archæological Journal'

the west end. The *confessio*, the result of the peculiar
conditions at Rome, is dropped; nor are aisles
required in such small churches as are at first built.
There is sometimes a central tower, in addition to
that at the west end.

Immediately after the Conquest a wave of Norman influence submerged the national tradition for
a time. The apse appears again; the central tower,
even when there are no transepts, is very characteristic of even the smallest churches; the western
door becomes more common. But it is chiefly in the
great abbey churches that the foreigner's hand is
most clearly seen. We have no great Saxon abbey
with which to compare those of the Normans, it is
true; but when we find how soon the Norman plan
was changed for one resembling that of the small
Saxon church, we shall recognize its exotic character.

It is in the eastern limb of the great cross-churches that we see the contending ideals of the two peoples. Two types of east end were introduced by the Norman Benedictines. In one the aisle is carried round the apse, and from it chapels project. This plan, which came to be called a *chevet*, continued, with modifications, to be the typical French ending.

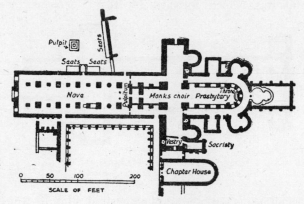

FIG. 131. THE CHEVET, NORWICH

Norwich may be taken as a good English example. The other, or Normandy type, has a Lombardic, and perhaps ultimately an Oriental, origin.[1] The aisles terminate in apses on a line with the chord of the great apse. Outside these, short aisles project from the transepts, and beyond these again other apses. St. Albans is given as an instance. Neither of these types, though expressed in examples so numerous and so vast, was to outlive three generations.

In accordance with the tradition of their past, and with what was to be their path in the future, the

[1] E. S. Prior.

English immediately lengthened the eastern limb,
and very soon too they showed a disposition to
return to their square east ends. At the beginning
of the thirteenth century, both in large churches and
small, they achieved both objects; they pulled down
almost all their east ends and rebuilt them both
longer and square-ended. The return to the square
end was helped forward by the Cistercians, on

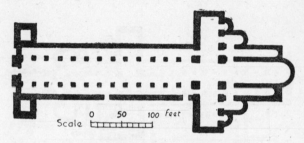

FIG. 132. PARALLEL APSES, ST. ALBANS
From Prior's 'Gothic Art in England'

whom it was imposed by their custom. But the Rule
—and this is noteworthy—though coming from
abroad, was chiefly, if not entirely, the work of an
Englishman, Stephen Harding. The Cistercians at
first built short choirs, as enjoined by the Rule but,
they presently gave way to the English love of
length. The central tower, though it unfortunately
disappeared from our smaller churches, became the
special glory of the cathedral and the abbey.[1]

But while the presbytery constantly grows longer
and longer, the nave attained its full length in early
Norman times. If afterwards a larger nave had been

[1] The bells were sometimes hung in a detached belfry,
as at Salisbury, Norwich, Chichester, and old Saint Paul's,
King's College, Cambridge, and various parish churches.

found necessary, the opportunity would probably have been taken to rebuild entirely the whole church. But so grand was the scale of the Norman buildings that this excuse could never be pleaded, and thus the Englishman's inclination to add to and improve rather than entirely rebuild was encouraged. In this way the Norman buildings gave the keynote. to work of a later period. This is especially notice- able in the proportions of the three storeys of the

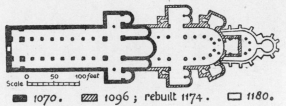

Scale 0 50 100 feet

■ 1070 . ▨ 1096 ; rebuilt 1174 . ☐ 1180.

FIG. 133. THE EXTENSION EASTWARDS
AND THE TWO TYPES OF APSE, CANTERBURY

building: main arcade, triforium, and clearstory. The Norman church still gave to the triforium that importance which it had inherited from the basilica. When a presbytery was rebuilt or lengthened the same proportions were preserved, so that the new work might range with the old. A tradition was thus established, which influenced English design even where, as at Salisbury, there was no earlier work to hamper the artist. Consequently in England the triforium dies hard. But it does gradually dwindle, is incorporated with the clearstory as a mere wall passage, and finally disappears.

The east end retained till after the Conquest something of the Basilican arrangement; the altar was placed somewhat in advance of the apse; behind it were ranged the seats of the clergy; the

9

central seat was considerably raised, and was
reached by a flight of steps, which projected in a
semicircle towards the west. The arrangement
probably continued till the general enlargement of
presbyteries in the thirteenth century, when the
seats were moved to the south side of the altar.[1] In

FIG. 134

THE AISLED APSE, ST. BARTHOLOMEW'S, SMITHFIELD. 1133

one instance only, namely, Norwich, are the remains
of the ancient throne preserved *in situ*. The extension eastwards gave space behind the high altar for
the more magnificent shrines which were then being
built to contain the relics of saints, such as St. Alban,
St. Cuthbert, St. Thomas à Becket, and for the
great crowds of pilgrims who visited them. Room
was also thus provided for additional altars, and
especially for the altar of Our Lady, which had

[1] J. T. Micklethwaite.

previously stood in the nave, or in some side chapel, but now was more sumptuously housed.

The monks' choir most often occupied the crossing; that of the canons the bays to the east of it. The screen which separates the choir and nave of these great churches varies in its details in different examples, but in its simplest form it consists of the following parts. (1) A cross wall against which the choir stalls are returned, and in

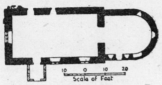

FIG. 135. BENGEO CHURCH

the centre of which there is a doorway. (2) A second wall one bay farther west, also with a central doorway. (3) The space between these two walls is covered by an upper floor forming a gallery or loft, called the *pulpitum*, supporting the great Crucifix or Rood and the organs. (4) A screen wall one bay farther west forming a reredos to the principal nave altar with a doorway at each end.

The parish church, like the cathedral and abbey churches, was generally rebuilt soon after the Conquest; it often still retains clear evidence of this in spite of the numerous alterations to which it has since been subjected. A church of this period has aisles if the size of the parish requires them, and though otherwise humble, it has very commonly a central tower and sometimes transepts, features which in later times are found usually only in the larger buildings. As we have already seen, both

central tower and transepts were to some extent
native productions, but their more frequent use at
this time is clearly due to Norman influence. The
church sometimes has an apse, but more often it is
square-ended.[1] The presbytery, as we have seen in
the churches of St. Augustine's mission, had formerly
been a part of the nave, merely enclosed by screens.
But it had now long since developed, both in France

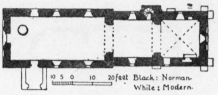

FIG. 136. STEWKLEY CHURCH

and in England, into a distinct chamber—a chancel;
the Norman only gave it a round end.

The parish church, as we see it to-day, preserves
in the most interesting language possible the history
of the people who have worshipped in it for eight
centuries. In some cases, it is true, one chapter
only of the story is told. Maybe the building of the
eleventh century, like Stewkley, is still sufficient for
the wants of the twentieth. Or, as at Sall,[2] a period
of prosperity has made possible an entire rebuilding,
which has given us indeed a complete work of art,
but has erased its earlier story. But far more often
does the building tell a tale of slow and continuous
growth. This growth took place in a remarkably
uniform manner over the whole country, though at
different rates in different districts. Thus the first
alteration or enlargement in any one church finds
its parallel in that of many others all over England;

[1] Figs. 135, 136.   [2] Fig. 138.

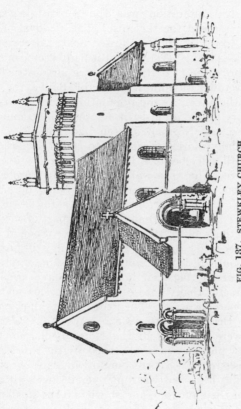

FIG. 137. STEWKLEY CHURCH

and in the same neighbourhood the change was not only similar in different buildings, but often contemporaneous.

The first alteration was the substitution of a square east end for the apse. The removal of the central tower generally followed next, the reason in some cases being perhaps that it had become unsafe, but more often that its piers were an obstruction. The new tower was almost invariably built at the west end of the nave. As the population grew, it became necessary to add an aisle, if, as was more commonly the case, the Norman church had not aisles.[1] It was usually more convenient to build the aisle on the north side, because there were more graves to the south. The aisle wall was built first probably, and then the arches were made, being often cut through the nave wall without taking it down. Thus it comes about that the upper part of the wall is sometimes older than the arches.[2] Soon it was found necessary to enlarge the building still further, and a south aisle was built in the same way; and so the arches between it and the nave are later in character than those on the north side and the aisle is perhaps wider. Then the north wall is moved out, so that the north aisle becomes the wider. If there were transepts in the Norman church, they had now probably been absorbed by the aisles. The wide aisle requires a corresponding increase of height, and a flat lead roof was put over it level with the eaves of the nave roof, and so we find the small early clearstory windows of the nave look into the aisle; a new clearstory was then built above the old one.

If the church was now becoming a large one transepts were perhaps again built, or the squire or a

[1] Fig. 139.   [2] As at Grantham and St. Nicholas, Leicester.

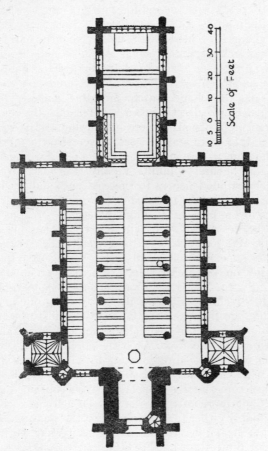

Scale of Feet

FIG. 138. SALL CHURCH

gild built a south wing as chantry chapel (now a family pew) with a squint hole through which the high altar could be seen. Sometimes the old chancel arch, though inconveniently narrow, was not rebuilt, but a small arch was cut through the wall on each side of it.[1] In the aisleless church there had been, at the end of the nave, on each side of the chancel arch, an altar enclosed by screens. Sometimes the altars stood against the chancel screen.[2] When aisles were added, these altars were moved into them and enclosed by screens; the marks of the screens are usually visible on the responds and on the first column. Finally, the aisles were often continued nearly to the east end, and arches made through into the chancel. One of the chancel aisles, or a part of it, was sometimes used as a sacristy, in which were kept the vessels and vestments and other things required in the service. When the chancel has not aisles, there often still remains on its north side a sacristy, which also generally contained an altar. There is sometimes a vaulted chamber below it, half underground, in which might be placed any human bones disturbed in making graves or in digging the foundations of any additions to the church. Over the porch there is very often a chamber communicating by a winding staircase with the church. Its uses seem to have been various; sometimes it appears to have contained an altar, but more often to have been a living-room, presumably either for a priest or for the guardian of the church, and it is not unlikely that it was used for occasional meetings and for other purposes.

[1] Fig. 140.
[2] At Guilden Morden, Cambridgeshire, the rood-screen and the screens enclosing the side altars still remain.

TWELFTH CENTURY

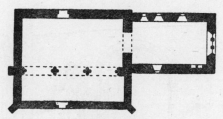

FOURTEENTH CENTURY

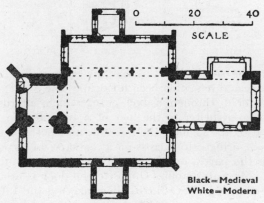

0   20   40

SCALE

Black = Medieval
White = Modern

FIFTEENTH CENTURY

FIG. 139. GROWTH OF THE PARISH CHURCH, COTON

At this point we may take a survey of the church, in order to notice several features and characteristics which have not found a place in the outline given above of its growth.

The church stands rather on the north side of the churchyard, and is entered generally from the south. There is a north door, somewhat plainer

FIG. 140. CHANCEL ARCH, SHEPRETH CHURCH

than the south, but this has generally fallen into disuse, and has often been filled up. The graveyard is entered through a lych-gate, which affords a moment's shelter to the bier at a funeral. To the south of the chancel there stood, and perhaps still stands, a high stone cross on a 'calvary' of steps.

In the porch, or immediately within the church, is a holy-water stoup. Opposite the door is a large wall-painting of St. Christopher carrying the Infant Christ across the river. The traveller uttered a prayer before the picture, for this act protected him during the day from the various dangers of the road.

The first object that would arrest attention was

the great representation of the Passion over the entrance to the chancel. The chancel screen filled the lower part of the archway, and supported a gallery or loft some six or eight feet wide. On the loft, or on a beam above it, stood the crucifix, with the figures of the Virgin and St. John on either side, and in many churches figures of angels. A great number of lights were burned on the loft on special occasions, and hence it was sometimes called the 'candle-beam'. Parts of certain services were sung from the loft by hired singers, accompanied by organs and other instruments. The Epistle and Gospel were not read from the rood loft, as is sometimes supposed, but from a lectern.[1] The whole of the chancel arch seems, in many instances, to have been filled up with a tympanum of boarding behind the rood, painted either with accessories to the scene of the Crucifixion or with a picture.[2] The lower part of the screen was panelled and painted with pictures of saints, and the whole of the screen was

[1] Micklethwaite. There is, however, some difference of opinion on this point.

[2] As at Wenhaston, Suffolk.

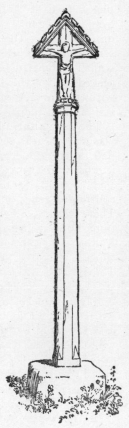

FIG. 141. CHURCHYARD CROSS, SOMERSBY

enriched with colour and gold. On the wall above the arch was a great painting of the Last Judgment.

Entering the chancel, which was generally level with the nave, we find the stalls for the priests are placed against the north and south walls and often 'returned' against the screen, that is, three or four on each side of the entrance have their backs to the screen and face eastwards; these are called 'return stalls'. Sometimes large earthenware jars were placed under the floor on which the stalls stood, with the object of improving the quality of the singing and increasing the volume of sound.

The high altar, placed close against the east wall, was of stone. It was covered with a linen cloth and had an embroidered frontal. There were commonly a cross and two candlesticks on the altar, or on a shelf behind it, and a reliquary, or silver vessel containing relics of a saint, but no vases of flowers. There was also a light kept constantly burning. Curtains hung from iron rods projecting from the east wall at either end of the altar, and there was sometimes a canopy over it and a curtain at the back. The reredos was either of stone or alabaster, with statues and scenes carved in relief and coloured, or it was a 'table with leaves', that is, a painted panel with doors, or a 'table' without leaves. In either case the painting was in *tempera*, colour mixed with yolk of egg, on a very thin coat of hard fine plaster called *gesso*. Over the altar hung the pyx, a silver vessel containing the Sacrament, under a tent-shaped canopy of linen or silk. In Lent a veil was drawn across the chancel in front of the altar.

In the south wall of the chancel are the three stone seats which we now call the sedilia, and a piscina for carrying off the water with which vessels were washed. There was seldom a 'credence' (Italian *credenza*, a side table), for the sacred vessels were, in England, placed at once upon the altar.

One of the most important ceremonies of the year was that with which the Easter Sepulchre was connected. The Easter Sepulchre was on the north side of the chancel, but it varied in form and character, in different churches, and was of varied

FIG. 142. EARLY SEDILE, STEWKLEY

degrees of enrichment. Sometimes an altar-tomb was used, and doubtless people often desired that their tomb should be on the north side of the

FIG. 143. MEDIEVAL SEDILIA, CHERRY HINTON

chancel in order that it might be so used. Often there was a permanent recess in the wall of architectural character. The service of the Easter Sepulchre at Durham was, briefly, as follows:

'Uppon Good Friday theire was marvelous solemne service, in the which, after the Passion was sung, two of the eldest monkes did take a goodly large Crucifix bringing it betwixt them to the lowest steppes in the Quire, and then one of the said monkes did rise and went a pretty way from it with his shoes put off, and verye reverently did creepe uppon his knees unto the said crosse and most reverently did kisse it. And after him all the other monckes, in the meantime all the whole quire singinge an himne. The service beinge ended, the two monkes did carrye it to the Sepulchre which was sett up in the morninge on the north side of the Quire nigh to the High Altar, and there did lay it, with another picture [*i.e.* statue] of our Saviour Christ in whose breast they did enclose the blessed Sacrament of the Altar, sencigne it and prayinge into it upon theire knees.

'There was verye solemne service uppon Easter Day between three and four of the clocke in the morninge, where two of the oldest monkes came to the Sepulchre and did sence it sittinge on their knees. Then they both rising came to the Sepulchre out of which they tooke a marvelous beautifull Image of our Saviour representing the resurrection, in the breast whereof was enclosed in bright christall the holy Sacrament, through the which christall the Blessed Host was conspicuous to the behoulders. Then after the elevation of the said picture, singinge the anthem *Christus resurgens*, they brought it to the High Altar. The which anthem beinge ended the two monkes tooke up the picture from the Altar, proceeding in procession to the South Quire dore, where there were four ancient Gentlemen belonginge to the Prior holdinge upp a most rich Cannopye of purple velvett, to beare it over the image carried by two monkes round about the church, the whole quire waitinge uppon it with goodly torches and great store of other lights, all singinge, rejoycinge, and praising God, till they came to the High Altar againe, whereon they did place the image, there to remaine untill the Ascension Day.'[1]

Before leaving the chancel, the westernmost window on the south side must be noticed. The sill is lower than the others, and the lights are divided

[1] *The Rites of Durham* (abbreviated).

by a transom. The upper part is glazed; the lower part had formerly no glass, but it was barred with iron and had shutters. Sometimes the window is on the north side, sometimes there is one on each side. What the object of this arrangement was we do not know. We can only say that there 'low-side-windows', as we call them now, were not for any of the purposes which they are commonly supposed to have served. They were not for the administration of the Sacrament to lepers, nor for lepers to stand at to see the celebration; nor were they to enable anyone to watch the light at the high altar; nor for confession. Most probably they were for ringing a small hand 'sanctus bell' to warn people outside of the moment of consecration of the Sacrament. Another theory, not perhaps impossible, has been put forward: that a light was placed in these windows to scare evil spirits from the churchyard.[1]

Near each altar are aumbries or cupboards in the wall, in which are kept the vessels used at the services; there is sometimes one especially high for the processional cross. The number of vessels used at the altar and otherwise, of course varied very much in different churches. A country church of average size had, perhaps, but a silver chalice and paten, a pair of laten cruets, a censer and a pair of candlesticks, for each of its three altars, with a few other vessels, and some half-dozen sets of vestments and altar coverings. A large town church, on the other hand, might have seven altars, a dozen chalices and patens, silver and silver-gilt, a score of other vessels, besides reliquaries, crosses and banners, crowns and other ornaments for images, perhaps forty sets of vestments, including copes

[1] J. F. Hodgson, *Archæologia Æliana*, xxiii.

embroidered with various designs and numerous altar frontals and linen cloths.

The church still, perhaps, retains one or more of its 'consecration crosses'. These were twelve crosses painted on the wall to mark the places anointed by the bishop at the consecration of the church. There were twelve more outside the building, but these have almost invariably disappeared.

FIG. 144. CONSECRATION   FIG. 145. CONSECRATION
CROSS, LANDWADE   CROSS, HEYDON, NORFOLK

Every church, probably even the very humblest, was adorned with large wall-paintings in *tempera*,[1] sometimes of very great beauty, of scenes from Scripture and from the legends of the Virgin and of the Saints, and allegorical subjects. These seem to have been more numerous in the eastern counties, while in districts where stone was abundant sculpture, which also was coloured, was more developed. In the fifteenth century a great quantity of sculpture of somewhat inferior quality was turned out of the alabaster works in Nottinghamshire. The wall-paintings, appropriately to their decorative scheme and to the possibilities of the process, seem to have been delicate and quiet in colour, and restrained in

[1] See page 110.

effects of light and shade. They contrasted strongly, in the former quality with the brilliance of the coloured glass. The windows contained subjects similar to those on the walls, or single figures, and in the tracery lights heraldic shields. They were often of a memorial character, and a small figure of the donor or person commemorated kneels at the feet of the saint and utters his prayer.

FIG. 146. PAINTED DIAPER, ST. CROSS

Probably the floor was most commonly covered with tiles, either plain or ornamented, though stone and other materials were used, and perhaps, in the humbler buildings, simply beaten earth and rushes. The decorated tiles were usually red, with devices of foliage, figures, grotesques and heraldry, in buff. They were made by deeply incising the pattern in the red clay, filling the hollows with a yellow 'slip', and then glazing and baking. Thus the design could hardly be obliterated, even by very long wear. Sometimes the pattern was simply incised.

The roof was decorated with a powdering of sprigs of foliage and sacred

FIG. 147
PAVEMENT OF INCISED TILES

monograms, few colours, and those subdued in tone, being used.

This survey of the medieval church may be concluded with a reference to some common mistakes. The popular theory about 'leper windows' has been already noticed. Another very persistent notion is that when the chancel is inclined at an angle to the nave it was intended to symbolize the drooping of our Lord's head as He hung upon the

FIG. 148
PAVING TILE,
VALLE CRUCIS

cross; but there is no shred of evidence that the builders had any such thought, and the inclination of the chancel to the nave is without doubt purely accidental. Another modern fancy is that the chancel was made to point towards the place on the horizon where the sun rose on the feast of dedication, or on the day when the building was begun. But almost every church stands nearly due east and west, whereas those dedicated to Saints Thomas, Stephen, John the Evangelist should stand south-east and north-west, while those dedicated to the Holy Trinity, St. Peter, and St. John Baptist should be north-east and south-west. Nor can it be supposed that all churches were begun at one of the periods of equinox, which the alternative view would require. The idea that early cross-legged effigies commemorate Crusaders is also devoid of foundation. It may also be mentioned that the helmets and swords placed on iron brackets over the later monuments are seldom the arms actually used by the person commemorated, but are almost invariably trophies used at his funeral.

We may now take up the history of the

church at the point reached before the foregoing digression.

The first of the changes in the churches during the sixteenth century was the destruction of the rood and of images, relics, and shrines, so that 'no remains or memory be found of them', in 1541. The suppression of the gilds and chantries by Henry VIII in 1545 and by Edward VI in 1547 caused the discontinuance of many services and the extinguishing of the lights which had been maintained by the payments of the gild brethren and by the chantry endowments. Candles were definitely forbidden by the Injunctions of 1547, except two upon the altar, and these appear to have been disallowed soon afterwards. 'A comely and honest pulpit' was to be provided, and the Epistle and Gospel read thereform or from other convenient place. The Royal Arms were to be put up. A copy of the Bible in English and a translation of Erasmus' *Paraphrase of the New Testament* were to be placed in every church. The order to destroy all shrines and coverings of shrines, and all pictures and paintings on walls or windows, was repeated. A chest for collecting alms for the poor was to be fastened near the high altar.

In 1550 some used 'the Lord's board after the form of a table, and some as an altar'. Orders were issued to destroy all altars, and to provide 'an honest table decently covered in such place of the quire or chancel as shall be thought most meet'. It appears that texts from Scripture were painted on the walls in place of the destroyed pictures, for in the reign of Queen Mary orders were issued (1554) that these should be obliterated. Fragments are occasionally found, confused with the earlier

paintings, under coats of whitewash. The old ornaments were of course restored under Queen Mary,
so far as was possible, with 'a rood of a decent stature,
with Mary and John and an image of the patron of
the same church'.

In the first year of Queen Elizabeth injunctions
very similar to those of Edward VI were issued.
And whereas some altars had been taken down
and others not, and whereas, 'saving for an uniformity, there seemeth no matter of great moment,
so that the sacrament be duly and reverently
ministered', yet for uniformity and convenience the
altar was to be removed and a table set in its place
and covered; 'and so to stand saving when the
communion of the sacrament is to be distributed;
at which time the same shall be so placed in good
sort within the chancel as whereby the minister
may be more conveniently heard of the communicants in his prayer and ministration, and the communicants also more conveniently and in more
number communicate with the said minister'. After
communion the table was to be replaced, At the
same time it was ordered that the old altar was not
to be taken down 'but by oversight of the curate
and churchwardens, wherein no riotous manner be
used'. Proclamation was also made forbidding the
mutilation of monuments, tombs, graves, or inscriptions in memory of the dead, or breaking images of
kings and others, or breaking images on glass windows without permission of the ordinary, or taking
down and selling bells or lead.

The open decay and ruin of churches at this time
(1560) is described in a letter issued by the Queen,
in which she instructs commissioners to determine
some means of reformation, 'and among other things

to order that the tables of the commandments may be comlye set or hung up in the east end of the chauncell.' The old service books were ordered to be defaced and abolished in the following year.

In 1569 Archbishop Parker issued inquiries as to whether baptism was ministered in a basin or in the font, and whether the Holy Communion was ministered in 'any prophane cuppes, bowles, dishes

FIG. 149
CHALICE AND PATEN
HAMSTALL RIDWARE. FIFTEENTH CENTURY

FIG. 150
COMMUNION CUP
SALL. 1568

or chalices heretofore used at masse, or els in a decent communion cuppe provided and kept for the same purpose only, and whether the communicants do use to receyve the holy communion standinge sittinge or els knealinge, whether the roode lofte be pulled down according to the order prescribed; and if the partition between the chauncel and church be kepte'. Many of the old chalices were inconveniently small now that the laity communicated in both kinds. A great number of companions cups and patens still in use bear the date 1569.

The position of the altar or communion table was still a burning question in the reign of Charles I. For one thing, it was taken, we are told, as an index of the character of the service. The puritanical party, regarding the service as a religious feast, wished to have the table brought from the east end into the body of the church when communion was to be celebrated, while those who viewed the celebration as a sacrifice wished the table to be placed

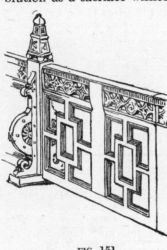

FIG. 151
ALTAR RAIL, MILTON. *c.* 1640

altar-wise at the east end. Decision was given in favour of the high-church party by Archbishop Laud. The latter gradually established a uniform practice in the matter, and he provided candlesticks, alms-basin, carpet, and other furniture, while Bishop Cosin even introduced a crucifix and censer into the chapel of Peterhouse in Cambridge. Laud also required that communion rails should be provided, 'near one yard in height, so thick with pillars that dogs may not get in', and he introduced from Italy the 'credentia' or credence. Pews were not to be much above a yard high, and the reading-desk was not to stand with its back to the chancel nor far from it. The fabric of the church also was repaired and furnished in a picturesque sort of Gothic style. Some curious window tracery, a number of pulpits, and a few good roofs of this period are still to be seen, but most of the work has been destroyed at the 'restoration' of the church to make way for what is considered more correct Gothic. Laud's party were also accused of taking down galleries, some of which had been built early in the seventeenth century, and of restraining the building of them in parishes which were very populous. But Matthew Wren, Bishop of Norwich, one of Laud's party, appears to have found it necessary to instruct his ministers to 'take order that there may not come above 300 or at most 400 communicants to one communion, for which occasion they are warned to have communions oftener'.

During the Civil War and the Commonwealth the ornaments and other improvements introduced by Laud, and also much of the older work which the first reformers had spared, were destroyed. The amount of damage done varies very much in different places according to circumstances. Where puritanism was strong, as in East Anglia, the destruction was very great, while some secluded villages escaped with comparatively little damage. But luck entered largely into the fate of buildings. At Westminster Abbey, for instance, it seems miraculous that so much is left.

After the Restoration matters improved, but the process of repair was very slow in the poorer villages, and for years afterwards many churches were reported to be in a state of ruin. Gradually, however, things were brought round, roofs were repaired windows mended, new communion rails made, and everything was overspread with a coat of decent whitewash.

But our churches have had to pass through yet another ordeal, from which they have not yet wholly emerged. They have had to undergo the dangerous and often fatal operation known as 'restoration'.

Probably more old work has been destroyed by this process during the last seventy years than by the fanaticism and neglect of the preceding three centuries. But this misfortune has generally been due to excess of zeal, and it must be admitted that probably at no previous period have church buildings generally been kept in such decency and order.

The musicians who had played in the rood-loft previous to the Reformation had been relegated to a gallery at the west end. They appear to have been superseded by the barrel-organ early in the nineteenth century. An organ or harmonium in a parish church must have been rare till 1850.

It appears that the systematic heating of churches began soon after the middle of the nineteenth century. There is no indication that churches were artificially warmed in the Middle Ages; the people kept themselves alive by wearing plenty of warm clothing.

A word may here be said about parish registers. There are some few dating from the early part of the sixteenth century, but the first order on the subject appears to be a royal injunction issued by Thomas Cromwell in 1538. Entries of all marriages, christenings and burials that had taken place during the week were to be entered after service on Sunday; and if this was not done a fine of three shillings and fourpence was to be paid, and the sum devoted to the reparation of the church. The register was to be kept in the church in a chest, of which the parson kept one key and the churchwardens another. Parliament reaffirmed the injunction in 1558. The entries were probably made on loose sheets of parchment or on paper, but in 1598 Convocation of the Province of Canterbury ordered that these should be copied into parchment books, and copying clerks were sent round to make the copies. These are generally the earliest documents preserved, the originals having been in almost every case destroyed or lost. Sometimes the copy is of earlier date than this order, many having been made in 1570. In 1598 it was ordered that a copy of the year's entries should be sent to the bishop of the diocese. The Act so often referred to in the registers, requiring that all persons should be buried in woollen, was passed in 1678. Allusion is made to it in a song of 1680:

'Let them damn us to woollen, I'll never repine
At my lodging, when dead, so alive I have wine.'

There is occasionally still to be found in a country church the common plough of the parish, and sometimes the fire-book for pulling down burning houses. The arms which every parish was bound to provide are preserved in one cathedral (Norwich), and perhaps in others, but they have been removed long since from almost every parish church.

CHAPTER V

MONASTERIES

THE Benedictines: church, cloister, chapter-house, dormitory, frater, guest-house, infirmary.
Cluniacs, Cistercians, Carthusains. Augustinian Canons. Gilbertines. Friars. Templars. Hospitals.

EACH of the religious orders[1] developed a special arrangement of its buildings, to which every house of the order adhered fairly closely. The plan of the church grew out of the common traditional plan, with variations to suit the views and ritual of each order; the arrangement of the secular buildings was dictated by the practical requirements of the Rule. The differences, whatever their origin, in most cases are confined to details. As the Benedictines were the first to develop a typical plan, and as their houses became more numerous in England than those of any other order, it will be convenient to describe fully the ordinary arrangement of one of these, and then to notice the points in which other orders departed from it.

Something has already been said of the Norman plan of the great Benedictine Church (p. 99). In the twelfth century the apse was discarded, but the transepts and the central tower were retained. The latter, indeed, became a special characteristic of the English church of the first rank. The presbytery was lengthened, and secondary transepts sometimes added, as at Canterbury and Durham. The presbytery and choir occupy a larger part in the monastic

---

[1] A list of the religious orders is given in an appendix.

than in the parochial church, and are more com-
pletely separated from the nave; in these respects
the churches of the canons hold a half-way position.
The west part of the nave formed in fact a separate

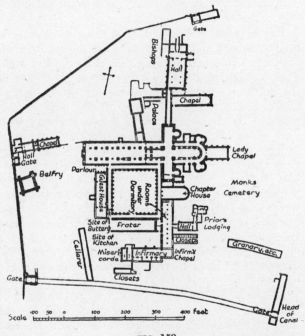

FIG. 152.

BENEDICTINE MONASTERY AND BISHOP'S PALACE, NORWICH

church for the servants and novices and for the
public; it was entirely distinct from the rest of the
building, had its separate entrances, and its principal
and smaller altars. The cloister and secular buildings
were placed on the south side of the church for the

sake of warmth, unless, as was often the case, some peculiarity of the site made it more convenient to put them on the north. Round the cloister were ranged the common buildings used daily by the monks, and beyond these lay various special buildings.

The cloister, which was the living-place of the monks, was at first covered by a simple lean-to roof, supported on stone columns standing on a low wall. Then a high wall with windows took the place of the columns, and the passages were often vaulted and covered with lead roofs. But the cloister long retained its character of a mere covered way with open sides. Gradually more shelter was obtained by glazing first the upper parts of the windows and then the whole. Finally, a series of little studies like sentry-boxes, and not very much larger, called 'carrells', were place against the windows. These were in use in the thirteenth century.[1] At Gloucester one side of the fifteenth-century cloister has recesses specially built to receive these carrells.

When the monks went to service they entered the church by a door in the north-east corner of the cloisters; each one as he passed placed the book which he had been studying in a large cupboard or *armarium* on the left of the door, or between the door of the church and that of the chapter-house. The recess for this cupboard may usually be seen; there is a good one at Ely. The cloister, in fact, formed the library, the reading-room, and the scriptorium, or copying-room, As books increased more presses were added. Sometimes a distinct library was built against the end of the transept [2] or elsewhere.

[1] J. W. Clark.   [2] Gloucester.

In another part of the cloister, sometimes the west walk, the novices were taught. The stone bench which runs round the cloister is often marked with little sinkings about the size of the bowl of a salt-spoon in groups of nine. These were doubtless for playing some such game as Nine Men's Morris, which still survives in our villages; but they do not appear to be confined, it must be confessed, to the novices' part of the cloister. There is another door into the church in the north-west angle of the cloister; it led into the part west of the pulpitum, and so would serve for novices and those who were not admitted to the choir.

In the east pane or walk of the cloister there is a series of doors leading into several buildings of importance. The first opens into a narrow space next to the transept, which was put to various uses in different houses—frequently a passage leading to the monks' cemetery. Next comes a large doorway, with a window on each side; this is the entrance to the Chapter-house. The normal shape for the chapter-house was oblong, either with a square east end,[1] as at Bury St. Edmunds, or with an apse, as at Norwich. The grand polygonal chapter-houses with which we are familiar were built chiefly in the thirteenth and fourteenth centuries, and for the most part by the great chapters of secular canons;[2] the vestibules through which they are entered are of great variety and beauty. Some few of the rectangular chapter-houses have also a vestibule, but usually there is none, and the entrance has not even a door.

[1] Figs. 155, 157.

[2] Lichfield, Salisbury, Wells, Lincoln, Hereford, Southwell, Beverley, York; also by the Benedictines at Westminster (Fig. 170) and Worcester.

Proceeding south, we come to the staircase which goes up to the dormitory, and then to a series of small rooms under the dormitory, such as the Common-house, or room in which great fires were kept burning in winter, to which the monks were

FIG. 153. ENTRANCE TO CHAPTER-HOUSE, ST. RADEGUND'S, CAMBRIDGE. *c.* 1180
From 'Cambridge Described and Illustrated'

allowed occasionally to go to warm themselves; a passage leading to the infirmary; in some cases a prison for refractory monks, and so forth. Over the whole of this range is the Dormitory. From it another staircase, in addition to that from the cloister, descends direct into the transept, so that when the monks rose for matins at midnight they could enter the church and return without going out into the cloister. At the south end of the dormitory and on the same floor is a large Necessary-house, containing a great number of closets divided by wood partitions. A stream of water was carried under it in an artificial cut. (Figs. 152, 155.)

To the south of the cloister stands the Refectory or Frater, the common dining-hall of the monks, entered by a doorway in the south-west angle of the cloister. It is usually on the ground floor, but is sometimes raised on vaulted cellars. Within the frater there is a lectern corbelled out from one of the side walls, from which one of the brethren read aloud, while the others ate in silence. The Lavatory, at which the monks washed their hands before and after meals (for fingers were made before forks), is in the cloister near the frater door. It consists of a long stone trough in a recess, and roller towels hung near by; there is a good example at Norwich. The Kitchen, in the greater houses at least, is often a large and lofty detached building at the west end of the frater; that at Durham is a well-known example. On the west side of the cloister there are usually the Guest Hall, and cellars used for storage and other purposes. Here also is commonly a Parlour, where monks might see their friends or deal with traders, and also the Cellarer's Hall, where the ordinary guests were entertained. The almoner who dispensed broken victuals to the indigent had his quarters near the gate.

The most important of the outer ring of buildings is the Infirmary for he aged and the sick and infirm. Those who had recently been bled were also admitted in order to recover their strength. Monks were very willing to undergo the periodical bleeding for the sake of the few days of luxury in the infirmary. The building is usually to the east of the cloister,[1] and connected with it by a covered way. It is planned

FIG. 154. REFECTORY LECTERN, CHESTER

like a church, with a rather long nave and aisles and by a cross wall with a doorway. The part to the west of this wall is the infirmary proper, and the part to the east formed, with the chancel, a chapel. The aisles were in later times often cut up into a series of small rooms by blocking up the arches and building

[1] The Westminster infirmary, built round a cloistered court (the charming Small Cloister), is abnormal.

cross walls. There was also a hall for those who could sit up to their meals.

The Misericorde was a hall which generally had some connexion with the infirmary, but its position and name vary in different monasteries; at Durham it was called 'the loft'. It was provided for those who were allowed to eat meat, and hence occasionally the whole convent dined there. As time went on these occasions became more and more frequent, till at last the frater was deserted for almost the whole year.

The palace of the bishop and the lodging of the abbot or prior gradually increased in magnificence, and included a large hall for the entertainment of the highest guests.

Besides all these there were great storehouses for grain and fish, mills and brewhouses and workshops, and the 'checkers' (exchequers) of the officers in charge of various departments of the establishment.

The Cemetery of the monks was usually to the east of the church. It was distinct from that of the lay brothers and the public. Burials were sometimes made in the church, in the chapter-house, in the cloister; never in the cloister-garth.

There were two hundred and sixty-seven Benedictine houses in England at the time of the Suppression.

Early in the tenth century an order of reformed Benedictines was founded at Cluny; hence they were called Cluniacs. They spread to England in the second half of the eleventh century, and at the Dissolution had thirty-two houses. They observed a very gorgeous ritual; their buildings were elaborately decorated, but did not differ very materially from those of the Benedictines.

II

The Cistercian order, another offshoot from the Benedictines, took its rise about 1100, at Citeaux (Latin, Cistercium). In its architectural development it is one of the most interesting and important of the monastic orders. The Rule, which was drawn up chiefly, if not entirely, by an Englishman, Stephen Harding, was one of extreme severity. Houses were to be planted in wild and desolate places. The smiling fields of Foutains and Tintern are evidence, not of the worldly wisdom of the monks, but of their skill and industry in agriculture. Manual work, as well as devotion and study, was required of the brethren; each establishment was to be self-supporting; to produce all that it required. It is due to this cause that towns did not grow up round their monasteries, as they did round those of the Benedictines such as Bury. Absolute simplicity was to be observed both in ritual and in architecture; hence the strongly marked characteristics which distinguish their buildings from those of other orders. There was to be but one tower, central and low, no unnecessary turrets or pinnacles, no triforium, no pictures on walls or in glass, crosses were to be of wood and candlesticks of iron.

The Church has a very short eastern limb (until lengthened in later times) with a square end. Chapels, divided by solid walls, project from the east side of the transepts. The monks' choir was in the crossing and the eastern part of the nave; the west part of the nave was the church of the *fratres conversi*, or lay brothers. These *conversi* formed a distinct and important class in a Cistercian house, where so many industries were practised. The aisles were separated from the nave by high screen-walls, against which stalls were placed.

The Chapter-house was square or oblong, and divided by columns and arches. The Refectory, which was similarly divided, was placed at right angles to the south pane of the cloisters, instead of

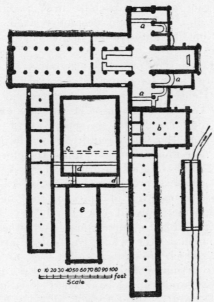

FIG. 155. CISTERCIAN PLAN, FURNESS ABBEY
SEE LIST OF ILLUSTRATIONS
From 'Trans. Cumberland and Westmorland Archæ. Society'

parallel with it. In other respects the secular buildings have a general resemblance to those of a Benedictine monastery. A small book-room is provided between the transept and the chapterhouse or between the cloister and the chapterhouse.[1] The self-supporting character and the

[1] W. H. St. John Hope.

isolated position of the houses necessitated more extensive outbuildings, such as mills and work-shops, then were required by the Benedictines.

The order was introduced into England in 1127, and spread rapidly, especially in Yorkshire. The severity of the life soon became relaxed. At the Dissolution 100 houses were suppressed.

The Carthusian order was founded in 1086 at Chartreuse, near Grenoble, whence they took their name. (Hence, also, the 'Charterhouse' in London and the 'Certosa' at Pavia.) The life was extremely ascetic, and not only was the separation of the com-munity from the world required, but the isolation of each individual. The buildings, therefore, differ radically from those of all other orders. A separate cell and garden is provided for each monk. On cer-tain days the brethren all dined together, but ordin-arily, they met only at the church services. The church, refectory, chapter-house, and other build-ings common to the whole community are small. The cells, which are really small houses, are ranged round a court and connected by a cloister. Between the houses and the cloister there is a corridor, accessible only to the Superior. Food was passed into each house through a hatch so contrived that the occupant could not see out through it. The house contains a living-room, a bedroom, a closet for keeping fuel (for the room was warmed by a fire in winter), and there was a garden in which the occupant might work. The order was introduced into England in the reign of King Henry III. The best-preserved buildings are those of Mount Grace, Yorkshire (about 1397). Eight houses were sup-pressed.

After the Benedictines the most numerous were
the Augustinians, an order of Canons living under
rule, and holding a half-way position between monks

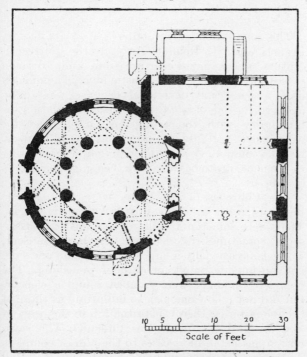

FIG. 156. CHURCH OF THE HOLY SEPULCHRE, CAMBRIDGE
From 'Cambridge Described and Illustrated'

and secular clergy; probably founded about 1100.
They had 170 houses.

The Gilbertine order, the only one of English
origin, was founded by Gilbert of Sempringham,

between 1131 and 1148, at Sempringham, in Lincolnshire. Monasteries were double, with a men's part
and a women's part. Twenty-six houses were suppressed by Henry VIII.

The foundation of the orders of Friars by St.
Francis and St. Dominic early in the thirteenth
century was a new departure from and, to some
extent, a reversal of the monastic idea. The monk's
life of study and devotional exercise was to be
changed for one of work for others; his isolation for
familiarity with the world; his confinement for
itinerancy. Not only the individual was to be poor,
but the community also. Preaching and ministering
to the poor was to be their work, begging their means
of support.

The Churches of the Friars were long, simple
buildings, with large naves for great congregations.
They were sometimes built without aisles or transepts, sometimes they had one very large transept.
There is occasionally a large open space on one side,
and an outside pulpit for outdoor preaching. The
domestic buildings were grouped round a cloister,
but did not follow one plan so uniformly as those of
the monasteries; their usual situation in the heart of
a town probably made this difficult. The same
reason has led in most cases to the almost complete
destruction of their buildings. Saint Andrew's Hall
at Norwich is the church of a Dominican house.

The only one of the Military orders whose buildings require notice is that of the Knights Templars.
The famous round church in London is said to have
been built in imitation of the church of the Holy
Sepulchre at Jerusalem. The other round churches

in different parts of the country were probably
founded with the same idea and under the influence
of the Templars.[1]

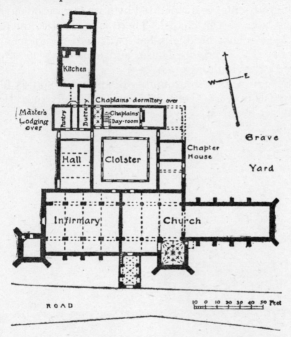

FIG. 157. THE GREAT HOSPITAL, NORWICH

The Hospitals, founded by the benevolent for the
aged and infirm, were arranged in various ways.
The example here given combines features of a
monastic infirmary and of a private house. The

[1] Holy Sepulchre, Northampton, about 1100–27; chapel
in Ludlow Castle, about 1120; Holy Sepulchre, Cambridge,
about 1130; Temple Church, London, finished 1185; Little
Maplestead, Essex, about 1300.

main building has the plan of an ordinary church, with aisles and transepts. In the nave and aisles were placed the beds; the eastern part, including the transepts, was separated by a wall from the nave, and formed the chapel. There is a cloister, out of which opens the dining-hall, with screens and butteries like a private house, and a master's lodging and other buildings.

There were also a number of special hospitals for lepers on the outskirts of towns. Usually only the chapel remains.

CHAPTER VI

HOUSES

NORMAN houses. Thirteenth century. Edward I: typical plan,
  growth of house, courtyards, gradual improvement.
  Shops, Tudor houses, changes in plan. Inns, play-acting.
  Inigo Jones. Eighteenth century.

OUR earliest domestic buildings date from the
twelfth century. After the Conquest stone was
more commonly used, and consequently several
houses of the Norman period have been preserved
to us. The stone-built houses in the towns which
still remain appear to have belonged in most cases
to Jews, the rich men of the period, and a class
which must often have found it necessary to have a
house that was capable of defence. The best known
are those at Lincoln, in which the principal rooms
are on the upper floor. It was a common plan, both
in private houses and in the secular buildings of
monasteries, to reserve the ground floor for offices
and storerooms, and to cover it with a stone vault,
supported on a row of columns running down the
middle of the building; the living-rooms, were placed
above, and were sometimes reached by an outside
staircase only. In some of the larger houses the
hall was on the ground floor, and was divided by
arches into a nave and aisles like a church.[1] Westminster Hall, built by William II, was thus divided
originally. Probably the columns were often of
wood, like those in the Bishop's Palace at Hereford.

Whether the hall was above or below stairs, it
occupied the greater part of the house. Hence the

[1] Fig. 152, Hall of Bishop's Palace.

application of the word Hall in very early times to the whole house. The only other rooms were a cellar at one end of the hall with a room over it and at the other end of the hall the kitchen offices.

Little building was done in the first half of the thirteenth century, but in the latter part houses

FIG. 158. NORMAN HOUSE AT LINCOLN

improved considerably, and the typical manor-house was then gradually developed. The same general arrangement was followed, but there was an advance in refinement and comfort and in the quality of the workmanship. Fireplaces became more common. Glass windows were still almost unknown, even in the king's own houses. The medieval story of King Arthur tells how 'there befell a marvellous adventure, that all the doors and the windows of the palace shut by themselves; but for all that the hall was not greatly darkened, and therewith they were all abashed both one and another'.[1] Here, to

[1] Sir Thomas Malory.

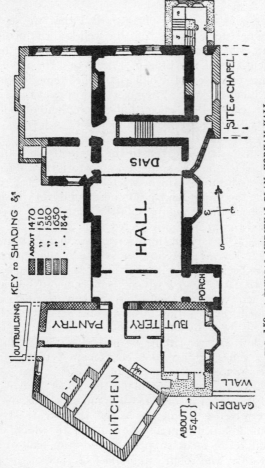

SCALE

10 5 0 10 20 30 40 FEET

KEY TO SHADING &c.

ABOUT 1470
,, 1510
,, 1580
,, 1650
. . . 1841

OUTBUILDING

PANTRY

BUTTERY

KITCHEN

ABOUT 1540

WALL

GARDEN

PORCH

HALL

DAIS

SITE OF CHAPEL

FIG. 159. A TYPICAL MEDIEVAL PLAN, HORHAM HALL.
From the 'Proceedings of the Cambridge Antiquarian Society'

close a shutter is thought of as closing a window.

It is in the reign of Edward I that we see the gradual development of the well-known medieval plan, which continued with but little change in its essentials till the time of Elizabeth. The medieval house consisted of a hall going the whole height of the building, with a wing of two storeys at each end. The hall had an open timber roof, and usually a central hearth. It was lighted from both sides, and on each side there was a door at the 'lower' end, which was that nearest to the kitchen. The 'upper' end of the hall was raised a step to form a dais for the high-table, which stretched across the hall, while the tables for the retainers ran down the sides. To check the draughts from the doors, shirt screens, called 'spurs', were projected from each of the side walls; afterwards a third screen was placed between them, leaving two intervals, which may perhaps have been hung with curtains; then the passage between the doors, which itself came to be called the screens, was ceiled over and thus a gallery was formed; finally the intervals between the three screens were fitted with doors, The bay, or oriel window, as we call it, is another development of later times; it formed a convenient retired corner when houses had so few rooms.[1]

The ground-floor room at the upper end of the hall was often a sort of storeroom or 'cellar'; over it there was the chamber or 'solar', the private sitting-room and bedroom of the family, to which they could retire after supper, leaving the hall to the servants. The room commanded a view of the hall through a small loophole. It had a fireplace with a

[1] For plans see Figs. 152 (palace), 159, 163.

projecting hood or mantel (whence our term mantel-piece) carried on corbels and sloping back to the wall. The window recesses were continued down nearly to the floor to form seats (Figs. 160, 161).

FIG. 160. A FIREPLACE
WITH A MANTEL. *c.* 1300

FIG. 161. WINDOW-SEAT
THE PALACE, SOUTHWELL

Large houses had a private chapel adjoining or near to the solar. In some cases a gallery extended over part of the chapel for the accommodation of the family, while the retainers sat below (Fig. 162).

Returning to the lower end of the hall: the end wall, beyond the screens, contained two doors, one opening into the buttery (the 'butlery'), the other into a passage leading to the kitchen and larder; frequently there was a third door to the pantry, where bread, butter, etc., were served out. The larder retained its importance till quite recent times, owing to the necessity of larding down large quantities of meat for the winter, while the beasts were

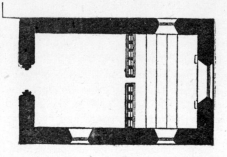

FIG. 162. CHAPEL IN A PRIVATE HOUSE, EAST HENDRED
From Turner and Parker's 'Domestic Architecture'

still fat. The rooms over the offices were probably
bedrooms for women-servants, the men sleeping, as
of old, in the hall.

The house was gradually enlarged by adding
room to room, especially by extending laterally the
wings at each end of the hall. In course of time

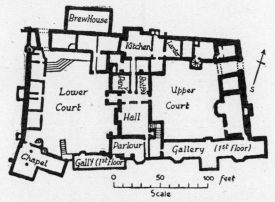

FIG. 163. TYPICAL HOUSE WITH TWO COURTS,
HADDON HALL

this led to the formation of a courtyard surrounded
by buildings, and sometimes of two courts, one on
each side of the hall. From these three stages of
development—the central hall with a projecting
wing at each end, the single court, and the double
court—the normal plan of later times was derived.
The smaller houses, of course, contained the simple
primitive arrangement more or less, according to
circumstances. They were almost always of timber,
as indeed were most of the larger houses except in
districts where stone was the more easily obtainable.
The overhanging of the upper storey was, perhaps,

an idea borrowed from the towns, where land was valuable, but it is a method of construction very suitable to timber, and also affords protection from the weather to the lower parts of the walls.

FIG. 164. HORHAM HALL

The only other changes made in this plan during the Middle Ages were in matters of detail, tending chiefly to the greater seclusion of the family. The solar becomes more important, and separate bed-rooms are provided. The upper rooms at each end of the house, formerly separated by the high central hall, are now sometimes connected by a gallery built out from the side wall of the hall. The staircase

remains an insignificant feature. Glass gradually
becomes more common, the window is divided by a
transom, the lower part having bars and a wood
shutter to open, the upper part having glass fixed.
Glass was considered to belong to the tenant till the

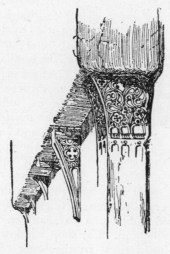

FIG. 165. ANGLE-POST AND BRACKETS,
BURY ST. EDMUNDS

time of Henry VIII; it was, therefore, sometimes
set in a wood frame which was fitted into a rebate
in the stonework and could be easily removed. The
walls were plastered and painted, the lower part
being sometimes boarded or panelled. In the fifteenth century tapestry was much used, but later
it gave way to the cheaper 'painted cloths' which
Falstaff recommended to Mistress Quickly as pre-
ferable to 'these fly-bitten tapestries'.

The town house was less susceptible of variety in plan than the country house. The lower storey was usually a shop, and there was a somewhat insignificant staircase at the back to the living-rooms above. The architectural treatment of the street front was often elaborate enough, as may be seen in such towns as Shrewsbury. Their overhanging storeys, supported by richly carved posts and brackets, are familiar to all.

FIG. 166. SHOP OF MEDIEVAL TYPE, NORTH ELMHAM

The medieval shop was a place where goods were made as well as sold, and the master, with his family and apprentices, lived in the upper storeys, not in the suburbs. The building was almost invariably of wood till the eighteenth century, and even then very often only a brick skin was put in front of an old building, so that many an old skeleton still remains behind. The shop window was fitted with two hinged shutters; the lower of these was hinged at the bottom, and was let down during the day into a horizontal position to form a table standing out in the street, on which were exhibited objects for sale; the upper shutter was hung by its upper edge, and was raised to form a pent-house roof to shelter the stall. 'With your hat pent-house like o'er the shop of your eyes,' says Moth, in *Love's Labour's Lost*. The door was like the stable door of the present day. This sort of shop front was general till the first half of the eighteenth century, when glass windows were gradually introduced.

Before leaving the town a few words may be added about the Town Hall. Its early name was the 'Tolbooth', and it was originally built as a booth, a mere roof on wooden posts, at which to collect market tolls. When a room was required as a place of meeting for the Gildmerchant or the Town

FIG. 167. GUILDHALL, PETERBOROUGH

Council, the easiest and most convenient way of providing one without encroaching on the market-place, the rents for which were of value to the town, was to build a chamber over the Tolbooth. And when in later times, the Town Hall was rebuilt in stone or brick, the same arrangement was kept. Thus it happens that so many of our old Town Halls are entirely on the upper floor, and have a space open to the market underneath. Some few have been developed by a similar process from the shelter built on posts over the market cross. Occasionally they are built solid from the ground like ordinary houses.

In the reigns of Henry VIII and Elizabeth, the larger country houses generally followed the court-yard plan. The plan of the smaller house, and some-times also of the larger, assumes the well-known E shape, commonly supposed to be an allusion to the Queen's name. Houses planned in the form of initials, or in some other fanciful shape, are, indeed, an occasional conceit of the time, as in the famous plan by John Thorpe:

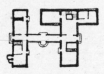

FIG. 168. THORPE'S PLAN FOR HIS OWN HOUSE. *c.* 1600

These 2 letters I and T
ioyned together as you see
Is ment for a dwelling howse for mee
                                        JOHN THORPE.

And no doubt the resemblance of the plan to an E would please the Elizabethan mind; but the arrange-ment is simply a central range with a wing at each end and a porch in the middle, a plan which has been common at all periods. This type continued till ousted by Italian ideas in the reign of James I.

The tendency in the sixteenth century was to abandon the closed courtyard. The insecure con-ditions of life which had led to its development no longer existed, and there was a greater demand for more light and air and for a 'prospect'. The fourth side of the court was therefore left open, or closed only by a wall with a gateway; thus the gateway came to be a detached building.

The rooms at either end of the hall are now

more conveniently, or at least more symmetrically, arranged. Though many rooms still open out of one another, and some rooms, even bedrooms, cannot be reached without passing through several others, they are ingeniously grouped and are connected by wide galleries, and numerous staircases are distributed about the buildings. The galleries occupy one side of a range, not the middle like a modern passage with rooms on each side. They are a development of the light covered ways which connected various parts of a large medieval building, and they form an important step towards the modern compact block of building as distinct from the medieval narrow and straggling range. The gallery built on the upper floor behind the hall, with small rooms or an open colonnade below it, becomes the great picture-gallery, which is one of the most striking features of the Elizabethan and Jacobean house. Its walls are panelled or hung with tapestry, the plaster ceiling has a rich pattern of panels and foliage, and the bow-windows give varied light and shade.

The hall has now become little more than an entrance-hall and lounge, though it retains its former grandeur and is still used for Christmas revels. The stately reception-rooms on the upper floor necessitated a corresponding enlargement of the staircase, which had hitherto been rather a neglected feature. It is still kept apart and separate from the hall. It is wide, massive, and richly decorated with carving. The screen, though often now of no use, is retained as an ornamental feature. Fireplaces have become universal in private houses, and splendid marbles and luxuriant carving are lavished upon them. It is only in a few college halls that the primitive central brazier and lantern in the roof are still used.

The Inns of the Middle Ages appear to have been poor and uncomfortable; the monasteries and the town and village gilds had supplied, and probably well supplied, the wants of the traveller. But the suppression of the monasteries and gilds brought about an improvement in the inns in the sixteenth century. The ordinary Elizabethan hostelry is built entirely of timber, and presents a street front similar to the ordinary house, except that it has a large archway leading through to a courtyard. The court is square, or more commonly long and narrow and it is surrounded by an open gallery at the level of each storey. The lowest rooms are offices; the bedrooms for guests are on the upper floors and their doors open on to the galleries.

These inn-yards were naturally chosen by the travelling showman, whether he led a dancing bear or a troop of acrobats, or performed sleight of hand, or what not, as his place of exhibition. For such a purpose its raised galleries made it extremely suitable. As the drama developed it too, of course, chose as its theatre the inn-yard. A rude stage was erected in the middle, with not even a background, far less with scenery. The 'quality' watched from the galleries, the 'groundlings' stood about in the yard. Burbage, in 1576, improved upon this primitive plan by moving the stage to one side and arranging a 'tireing house' behind it, while the part of the gallery which ran behind the stage was useful in the balcony scenes such as that in *Romeo and Juliet*. The absence of a curtain is illustrated by the invariable rule that in the tragedies the bodies of the dead

are carried away by the survivors.[1] And thus to
some extent the old inn-yard influenced the arrangement of the modern playhouse. Plays were, however, also given at Whitehall Palace, in the halls of
Colleges and of the Inns of Court, and in the palaces
of the nobles. The performances took place in the
great hall, and the arrangement of this had a larger
share in the development of the early theatre. The
stage was at the lower end of the hall, and the
gallery over the screens served for the balcony
scenes; the two doors in the screen long survived as
features at the back of the modern stage.

Inigo Jones broke entirely with the traditions of
the past in his plans, as in his architecture. The
house becomes a solid block instead of a narrow
range with numerous projections and broken outline.
The older plan was, indeed, continued at the same
time, till all building was stopped by the Civil War.
But when architecture revived at the Restoration,
the house of Elizabeth and James had disappeared.
All the reception-rooms, as they were now called,
were placed on the upper floors, and they certainly
were arranged with much more regard to state
receptions and architectural effect than to comfort.
The offices were placed in a basement below them.
The main floor was reached by a wide flight of stone
steps outside the house. The inside staircase,
leading only to the bedrooms, is treated as simply
as possible.

For the largest class of country house the favourite
plan of the eighteenth-century architects consisted
of a central block connected with low advanced
lodges by quadrant galleries. These advanced

[1] Pointed out by my friend Mr. Arthur Gray.

wings usually contained on one side the laundries and so on, and on the other side the stables. The reception-rooms were often effectively grouped, but the arrangement of the bedrooms is still defective. The exigencies of perfect symmetry and 'exact

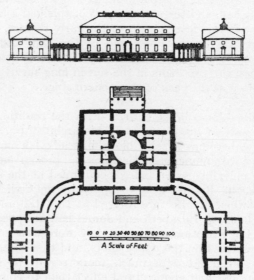

FIG. 169. THE EIGHTEENTH-CENTURY PLAN
GOODWOOD, SUSSEX

architecture' often rendered the lighting and ventilation of some rooms an impossibility. We have to thank the Gothic revival for throwing over the restraints of pedantic classicism, and for opening the way for a further advance in the art of house-planning.

CHAPTER VII
CONCLUSION

FRENCH and English, apse, proportions. Summary of history.
   Local varieties of style and workmanship.

GREAT and immediate as was the effect of the
Norman Conquest on English architecture, it was,
as we have seen, in many respects transient. Owing
to political and economic causes an extraordinary
impetus was given to the building of churches and
castles, and probably to that of houses. But artisti-
cally the country soon began to take its own way,
and ran its course, giving now and then a trial to
some suggestion from abroad, and generally dropping
it.

This English independence of French influence
has nothing to do with the relative merits of the
two national styles. Into that artistic and æsthetic
question this is not the place to enter. Merely is the
historical fact recorded that each country followed
its own bent. The fact that the two, under similar
conditions, often travelled nearly parallel paths, was
but natural. That the two paths so often diverged
is the more remarkable point, and a sufficient proof
of independence. While France was throwing her
great vaults at such immense heights England was
developing her entirely national open timber roofs,
and when she did make a florid vault she did it in
quite a different way from the Frenchman. And so
with window tracery. Through the thirteenth
century there was a general similarity, and perhaps
some borrowing, but in the fourteenth century the

155

national temperament began to tell. As our neigh-
bours grew more exuberant we became monotonous.
The English cannot be florid nor can the French
be dull, and when they became Flamboyant we
invented Perpendicular.

And as in the details of the craft generally, so in
church architecture in particular. Sir Gilbert Scott
has pointed out that on four several occasions was
the apse introduced into England, and four times
was it abandoned: we see it used in the church of
the Roman occupation, and in the church of St.
Augustine's mission, the Norman Conquest made it
for a time the almost universal fashion, and finally
at Westminster it was exemplified in a building of
surpassing beauty, and with all the prestige of a royal
foundation.

In the west front also is shown the tendency to
dwell on the horizontal line in contrast with the
French love of height. The end is spread out into
the western transepts of Ely and Bury; or a great
screen with rows of niches for statues is stretched
across as at Salisbury and Wells; or twin towers,
low and wide, are subordinated to the emphasis
placed on the broad unbroken front of Lichfield.
And most clearly of all is it shown in the long, low
roof-ridges of Winchester and St. Albans in contrast
with Amiens and Paris.

Right or wrong, we remain intensely insular. It
is perhaps our strength and our weakness that our
aims were always characteristically modest and
even humble. Under the influence of the Norman
we laid down immense buildings; we never surpassed
them. The largeness of conception of that time,
combined with the rudeness of execution, has the

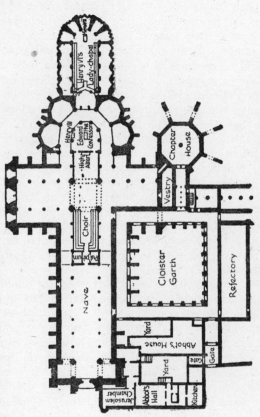

FIG. 170. THE FRENCH PLAN: WESTMINSTER ABBEY

SCALE: Three-quarters of an inch to one hundred feet

impressiveness of the work of giants. The interior of the nave of Durham, the western transept of Ely, both inside and out, the central tower of St. Albans,—these are rough-hewn epics which dwarf the efforts of later days. The lavish concentration of telling but barbaric ornament at salient points with the bold acceptance of the plain surfaces between, and the somewhat unwieldy bulk,—these early characteristics are refined down to the perfect union of beauty and strength in the choir of Canterbury.

The last traces of the Romanesque origin of our architecture were discarded by 1200, though there was still much to be done in refining and perfecting. If the builder of the thirteenth century was not quite so heroic as his forefathers, if he accepted the lines laid down by them as regards scale and breadth of treatment, at least his detail is unsurpassable for abstract beauty, for purity of line and cleanness of modelling, for absolute appropriateness and unity with the structure; witness Salisbury, Westminster, Lincoln, Beverley, Wells.

As the fourteenth century advances the builder becomes more deliberate and scholarly. His work is in some respects more elaborate and in others it is simpler. There is a more conscious aim at unity in the whole. As the window and niche are elaborated the decoration of the wall is suppressed, the bold wall arcades become superfluous. There is extraordinary ingenuity, but there is a loss of strength in the structural forms, and the carved foliage, beautiful and skilled as it is, has, both in its form and disposition, much of the character of a parasite. The Black Death, coming as it did when the art had already lost something of its vitality, undoubtedly had a numbing effect.

Towards the close of the fourteenth and during the early part of the fifteenth century, there was a reaction against the florid and somewhat limp style. King Henry VI, whose building schemes show great architectural power, gave expression to the feeling when he wrote, 'And I wol that the edificacion of my same Collcgc proccdc in large fourme clene and substancial, settyng a part super-fluite of too gret curious werkes of entaille and besy moldyng.'[1] But in general it was a reaction due rather to lack of energy than to restraint. Moreover, painting and sculpture began to assume the first place, and architecture proper to drop into the role of handmaid where she had formerly been mistress. An elaborate scheme of colour allows, and even demands, a corresponding simplicity of form, and as painting of wall and window advanced, architecture was forced to retire. The masses become attentuated and the foliage lifeless.

But the decline was not rapid. After the development of Perpendicular there came a period of rest under the Lancastrians, till the Wars of the Roses extinguished alike medieval life and medieval art.

The sixteenth century was an age of great house building, but it cannot be called an age of great architecture. The dead Gothic lingered on, tricked out, under the influence of foreign workmen, in classical details arbitrarily applied and classical ornaments of ugly and inappropriate form. But the builders retained enough artistic instinct to weld to some extent these elements and to produce buildings full of charm and character. During this period classical architecture made little progress, and it was not till the appearance of Inigo Jones that the

[1] Willis and Clark.

influence of the Italian renaissance was felt in this country. Inigo Jones gave a new direction to English architecture, which has influenced it ever since. And he introduced not only the new style, but a new system in the production of a building. Inigo Jones was the first English architect. Henceforth the common traditional knowledge of the crafts was to count for less, and the learning and power of one controlling mind for more. Inigo Jones's own work was a protest against the florid Elizabethan, and he set down his opinion in words which read almost like a paraphrase of Henry VI's protest against florid Gothic: Architecture should be 'solid, proportional according to the rules, masculine and unaffected'.[1]

Wren carried on the art of his predecessor in his own manner. But Renaissance architecture was to follow the course of medieval architecture, and indeed of all arts; it had its rise and its decline, and after Wren's time architecture slowly died, and a long series of importations and 'revivals' have failed to bring it back to life.

English architecture preserves its broad national characteristics over the whole country to a remarkable degree. There are, however, many local variations in matters of detail, both artistic and structural, due to several causes. Geographical and geological formations have been perhaps the most important. Political, economic, or social conditions have had considerable effect. Possibly, too, racial traits remained sufficiently distinct to account to some extent for the differences between the buildings of Yorkshire and Hampshire, of Norfolk and Devon.

[1] Blomfield.

The religious orders certainly had an influence on architecture which may still be traced; thus, the Benedictines were stronger in the east and south than elsewhere; the canons chiefly occupied central England; these settled districts were not suited to the Cistercians, whose greater houses were consequently for the most part in the wild regions of Yorkshire and the borders of Wales.

A district which was brought under cultivation at an early period, and whose population has remained agricultural and has not varied greatly, has numerous small churches very much in their original state, or at least not very much enlarged. In other parts the church has grown gradually with the population. In the towns and in the rich wool-growing or weaving districts, such as Somerset, East Anglia, and Coventry, many of the churches have been entirely rebuilt on a magnificent scale. In East Anglia, too, the influence of the Netherlands is seen in its paintings, in the stepped gables of the houses, and in its early use of brick. French influence is discovered in the south-east, and the ancient alliance between France and Scotland had a marked effect on Scottish architecture, as we see in the flamboyant tracery of Melrose.

But perhaps the most obvious of local peculiarities are due to the causes first mentioned, namely climate and geological formation, giving rise as they do to abundance or scarcity of particular materials, and hence to the use of particular methods of construction. In these days of rapid travel and of easy transport of material there is a general uniformity of style over the whole country. But in early days this was not so. In even the most important buildings it was necessary to use materials which could be obtained in the neighbourhood or in some locality with which there was fairly easy communication. The varying qualities of these local materials demanded different modes of treatment.

A great ridge of very good building stone runs in a broad sinuous band from Somerset, through

FIG. 171. WINDOW TRACERY IN A HALF-TIMBERED HOUSE,
OSWESTRY
PROBABLY FIFTEENTH CENTURY

Gloucester and Wiltshire, Oxford and Northampton, Lincoln and Yorkshire. This is, accordingly, the line of masonry and sculpture: witness the towers of Somerset and the spires of Northampton, the fine technique of Salisbury and the grand masses of Lincoln, the imagery of Wells, Worcester, Salisbury, Lichfield, Lincoln, the foliage of Southwell and of many a small midland church, the great palaces of Montacute, Wollaton, Burghley, Rushton, Went-worth, and the many admirable stone-built houses

FIG. 172. PART OF THE PALACE OF THE STANLEYS,
CHESTER

PROBABLY c. 1600

of the humbler sort. Hereford, Shropshire, and
Cheshire, with an abundance of soft, warm sandstone developed quite a distinct manner in their
churches, while their forests gave them the elaborate
half-timbered domestic architecture for which they
are famous (see Frontispiece).

FIG. 173. ROUND FLINT TOWER
BARTLOW
FOURTEENTH CENTURY

The monks of Ely, on the eastern border of the
midland district, could command its stone and its
sculpture; or, availing themselves of their native
chalk, produced the delicate 'pictures' and ornaments of their chapter-house. But East Anglia
possessed no durable stone, and the only building
material was flint. The stone necessary for doors,
windows, and angles had to be carried at great cost,
and was used with strict economy. Sometimes the
church towers were made round to save the expense
of getting stone for the quoins. Brick was largely

used in the middle of the fifteenth century—a hundred years before it became common in other parts—and was not rare a hundred years before this. The necessity of making stone go as far as possible led to a system of decoration which became very characteristic of the district; namely, that of stone and flint cut so as to form traceried panels and inscriptions. This parsimony in the use of stone produced a somewhat wiry style, and such a hard and disagreeable surface as that of a split flint should be kept very much in reverse.

FIG. 174
STONE AND FLINT,
SWANINGTON
FIFTEENTH CENTURY

The eastern counties, not having the materials for masonry or sculpture, turned their energies to carpentry and painting, and produced the wonderful roofs and screens of the Norfolk and Suffolk churches with

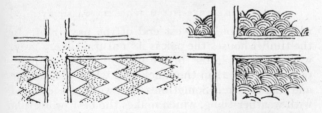

FIG. 175. PATTERNS IN STAMPED PLASTER, ESSEX

their elaborate paintings. There does not, however, appear to have been an elaborate timber domestic architecture. The woodwork was simple, or was entirely concealed. The decoration is usually done in plaster, divided up into panels, which are filled either with a simple stamped pattern or with elaborately modelled figures and foliage.

The south-east was another woodland district, and had some points in common with the west. Church spires are framed of timber, and are covered with oak shingles. The smaller churches often have a small timber bell-turret, with a low pyramidal

FIG. 176.   WEATHER-TILING, HOUSE IN SALISBURY

roof perched on the west end of the nave roof. In the timber houses the oak is its natural silvery grey, with yellow plaster between, which has a more pleasing effect than the black and white of Cheshire and Lancashire. Sometimes the walls are covered with weather-tiling, which makes the best protection against driving south-west winds.

The traveller cannot fail to notice other local varieties, some more, others less important than those glanced at above. Many of them may be studied in the humblest buildings, and thus they give an added interest to every village and country town.

APPENDIXES

I.—THE NINETEENTH CENTURY

HITHERTO the history of English architecture has been a story of order and discipline, of continuity and of movement. At times continuity may appear to have been strained, as in the middle of the sixteenth century, when foreigners were bringing in details based on the Roman Orders, or fifty years later, when Inigo Jones was showing how those Orders should be used. Movement was not always on the upward grade. Discipline may have been slighted by architects under Laud or may have degenerated in the eighteenth century to that of the barrack yard. But at any one time there had been one general style practised by all and applicable to buildings of every kind. The rudiments of the art had been based on tradition, and although new features had from time to time been imported from abroad they had been quickly assimilated and had become a part of the common national manner.

But the nineteenth century changed all that. During its course six or eight styles were used, without counting minor variations. And though fashion fluctuated most of these were in use at the same time. Almost every architect at one time or another ran through the whole gamut and in some cases was actually playing on all the instruments at once. He might be building at the same time a Norman and a Perpendicular church, a Jacobean house and an Italian bank, and possibly even using more than one style in the same building. A client might not know till he saw the plans that his house was to be in the Tudor style, but he would perhaps discover with surprise when it was finished that that applied to the outside only, the interior being pure Greek. Whether or not the national genius was equal to the strain thus

167

put upon its architects, the public seem to have been satisfied, and if there was anything still left to wish for it was expressed in the not uncommon question: 'Why

FIG. 177. CENTRAL CRIMINAL COURT, LONDON

don't you invent a new style?' But treating the most important of the arts in this fancy-dress ball style can hardly be considered a healthy symptom; for if art is the expression of a people and of a period it would seem that the most conspicuous characteristic of nineteenth-century England was that it did not know its own mind. It ultimately arrived at one definite if not very logical decision: that the architecture of Sundays and week days must be different.

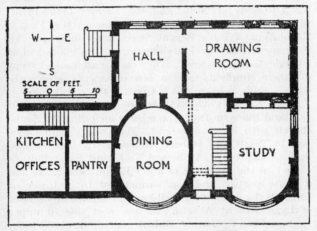

FIG. 178. A HOUSE-PLAN OF 1800

A few words may be said on the sequence of events by which this state of affairs was brought about.

English architecture, at least since the days of Wren, had been based on a well-organized body of Roman details which were fairly familiar to architects and builders alike. Perhaps it would have been wise to let well alone. But before the middle of the eighteenth century there was manifested a desire for the purer forms of Greece. Then, in 1763, Stuart and Revett published the first volume of their *Antiquities of Athens*, an instalment of the results of four years' study in Greece. The effect was remarkable. Greek art became the fashion, and Stuart was employed by the nobility to build houses in the Greek style. There followed a general movement in favour of extreme simplicity in architecture, in furniture, and in dress. Robert and James Adam are its best-known exponents, and Boodle's Club (1775), St. James's Street, in their manner, is a good example. The style degenerated into that called after the *Directoire* (1793-9), and the *Empire* (1799-1815), which characterizes the period following the French Revolution. Nash's Regent Street is an instance. All these men treat Greek architecture with a good deal of latitude, to say the least. They use the arch and, except for their simplicity and a few ornaments arbitrarily chosen, there is little that is Greek in their buildings.

John Nash (1752-1835) began Regent Street and Portland Place in 1813 the scheme including All Souls' church with its circular end. The County Fire Office was by Nash and Robert Abraham. In 1820 George Stanley Repton (d. 1858) and Nash built Saint Philip's chapel on the west side of lower Regent Street. It had a Doric portico and was surmounted by a tower or turret in the form of the well-known Choragic Monument of Lysicrates at Athens. On the west side of upper Regent Street Charles Robert Cockerell (1788-1863) built Hanover chapel with a portico over the pavement. Both these churches have been removed. Saint Pancras church in the Marylebone Road was built by William Inwood between 1819 and 1822, at a cost of over £60,000 exclusive of the organ and fittings. This building reproduced as closely as possible the Erechtheum at Athens, caryatid portico and all, and the absurdity of the thing is said by Fergusson to have done more than anything else to bring about the Gothic Revival.

The country had never for any long time lost its love of medieval architecture, which had in some sort been kept alive in the Cotswolds and other quiet country places all through the sixteenth and seventeenth centuries. One suspects that Shakespeare felt its charm.

There was something of a revival under Archbishop Laud, when much good work was done: Jesus Hospital at Bray was founded in 1627. Again in the time of Charles II some by no means despicable imitations were made, curiously mixed with the classical manner of the time, as in the Deanery at Winchester. The committee for rebuilding Saint Paul's hankered after something Gothic though they did not quite know what, and Wren himself essayed Gothic more than once. A ruin 'midst its dreary dells aroused a sentiment (generally false) in men like the poet William Collins, and before Collins's death Horace Walpole had, in 1750, resolved upon his Gothic castle at Strawberry Hill in Twickenham. Thus right down to the days of Scott with his Abbotsford, and Palmerston with his emotions on entering Westminster Abbey ('Damn it! Sir, I'm all devotion'), Gothic architecture every now and then reasserted its claim. And so it is not surprising that, when the romantic revival of the early nineteenth century took place, there was a general willingness to throw off the dull conventions and artificialities of Classicism in architecture no less than in literature.

But it must not be supposed that this occasional stirring of the dry bones meant that there was a spark of life left. Gothic architecture was as dead as a door-nail. There was profound ignorance alike of its technique, of its spirit and of its history. And thus while every builder had a rough working knowledge of Roman architecture as practised in England, just then undergoing a refining and at the same time a corrupting influence by the introduction of Greek models, architects had to begin a study of Gothic (far the most complex architecture that has ever existed) from the very beginning, without the aid of masters or of books.

In 1817 Thomas Rickman published his *Attempt to Discriminate the Different Styles of Gothic Architecture* and it was he who invented our present nomenclature of 'Early English', 'Decorated', and 'Perpendicular'.

Augustus Charles Pugin (1762–1832) began to issue his *Examples of Gothic Architecture in England* (three volumes of admirable measured drawings) about 1832, and his son, Augustus Welby Northmore Pugin (1812–52), published his *Contrasts*, his *True Principles*, and his *Apology for the Revival of Christian Architecture* between 1836 and 1843. The books are pleas for Gothic and, it may be admitted, lay down some common-sense principles. The early enthusiasts, it is to be noted, claimed Gothic as distinctively Christian, although it was practised for only four of the eighteen centuries of Christianity. Both Rickman and the younger Pugin were much employed in designing new churches.

In 1849 Ruskin published his *The Seven Lamps of Architecture*, an eloquent over-straining (when not a misapplication) of sound principles. He took great personal interest in the building of the Oxford Museum in 1854 by Deane and Woodward, the latter of whom was much influenced by Ruskin's teaching. In this building a first attempt was made to restore to the craftsman some of the artistic independence which he had enjoyed in the Middle Ages. Ruskin is partly responsible for the introduction of Italian features into England. His weight was entirely on the side of Gothic and of early Gothic: for Classic was stupid, Perpendicular corrupt, and Renaissance wicked. He had some influence on contemporary architecture—not directly, for most architects rejected his narrow dogma—but indirectly through his influence on a few of the profession and with the public. He did much to overthrow the stupid old stucco conventions and to establish a more sane and natural system of building. He was far in advance of his time on the subject of restoration.

The new style finding such favour, it behoved all architects to look about them, and even the old classical men had to fall into line. John Nash, the architect of Regent Street, also built Gothic houses and employed his assistant, the elder Pugin, in making careful studies of old examples which might serve as a basis for his own work.

In the new buildings of King's College, Cambridge (1822), William Wilkins (1778–1830) deserted the Greek of Downing College (1807–11) and the Grange in Hampshire (1809), for a Gothic design. In the Hall of King's the style is preserved throughout, but in the Provost's Lodge it changes immediately one crosses the threshold from the period of Henry VII to that of Pericles. The Gothic style was perhaps adopted at the instance of the College authorities. The scheme included the Gothicizing of Gibbs' fine Fellows' Building, but this part was happily dropped. Wilkins returned again to Classical architecture in London University College (1828) and the National Gallery (1832). It is fair to say that the latter is a mutilated design and does not do justice to Wilkins.

Meanwhile the Gothic stalwarts were carrying all before them. James Wyatt (1746–1813), who may be called the pioneer of the Gothic revival, had built the nave of Hereford Cathedral in 1786 and Fonthill Abbey in Wiltshire for Beckford in 1795. He had played fast and loose with Salisbury, Lincoln, Durham, and other cathedrals. It is curious to note how much Gothic art was destroyed by its early admirers. At Windsor Castle Wyatt's son, who became Sir Jeffry Wyatville (1766–1840), swept away much Tudor work and restored everything to true Edwardian (1824–30). Great as was the damage he did, it must be conceded that his work is at least simple and straightforward, and that he did not allow himself to be corrupted by the effeminacy of his royal master. The Round Tower, too, owes its familiar and effective silhouette to Wyatville. He added thirty feet to the height of its walls, and although the new work is a mere shell enclosing nothing, it is generally admitted that the appearance of the Tower must have been thereby greatly improved.

One feature of the Oxford Movement of 1840 was a protest against the drowsy cushioned comfort of the typical church, or at least of that part of it occupied by the gentry. Gothic architecture fell in with this protest. At first the energies of the Churchmen were directed to the work of restoring medieval churches. In these days and for long afterwards 'restoration' meant removing not only all work that was not Gothic but a good deal of medieval architecture that was 'debased': a term commonly applied to the work of the fifteenth century. This process continued unchecked for about forty years. Sir Gilbert Scott, a Gothic architect of great enthusiasm, became the autocrat of the movement, and in the course of a long and laborious life restored almost every cathedral and some hundreds of churches. The governing idea of the restorers was to bring back a building to its original state by removing all later work. At last, about 1878, when the process of restoration was about to be applied to the old church of Burford, William Morris was able by a happy accident to make a private, but characteristically vigorous protest, and to save the building. He forthwith founded a 'Society for the Protection of Ancient Buildings': i.e. protection from over-restoration. Morris's Society has been nicknamed the Anti-scrape Society on account of its protests against scraping the old face off the masonry and removing the plaster from the walls: a process which has doubtless destroyed acres of medieval wall-paintings which were hidden by whitewash, to say nothing of the stonework. The removal of plaster was based on the false notion that plaster is inconsistent with medieval architecture. The idea still lingers. Hence the plaster has lately been hacked off the nave vault of Durham Cathedral. But the notion of exposing stonework is entirely nineteenth century and almost entirely English, never held at any previous period of the world's history and rarely in any other country. The madness of mutilation gave its expiring and its most disastrous convulsion at Saint Albans Abbey towards the close of the century, when Lord Grimthorpe, a lawyer of great ability and great wealth, and expert on clocks, but an amateur architect totally devoid of capacity, destroyed much medieval work of various periods and substituted designs of his own.

In the thirties and forties the revival of religious zeal and the increasing prosperity of the country led to the building of a good many new churches. The new public schools which were being founded at the same time by groups of good churchmen had to conform to the patterns of Wykeham and Henry VII. New public buildings were to be built in the same style when required by historical associations.

In 1834 the old Houses of Parliament were destroyed by fire. The buildings had formed a royal palace from very early times, but had been so much altered and mutilated that little medieval work was visible. The Commons sat in what had been the King's Chapel, a costly and beautiful building with exquisite sculptures and paintings, the remains of which were hidden by panelling and fittings of the eighteenth century. Westminster Hall, which the fire had spared, had been simply the great hall of the palace. Historical propriety, therefore, combined with the fashion of the day in demanding a national and medieval style for the new Houses. The conditions for the competition of architects required that the style should be 'Gothic or Elizabethan'. The prize was awarded to Charles Barry (1795–1860). The river wall was begun in 1837, the building itself in 1840, and the Houses were formally opened in 1852.

The Houses of Parliament were the most important architectural work undertaken in the nineteenth century, and the most successful. Masterly in planning, both in the arrangement of the various parts and in the adaptation to the site and to Westminster Hall, they combine in a high degree the monumental symmetry of the great buildings of ancient Rome with the flexibility and freedom of the Middle Ages. In the elevations the dignified silhouette is maintained by preserving the unbroken vertical line. The chief fault is the monotonous repetition of the panelling, and the want of relief and contrast by broad plain surfaces. Barry secured the invaluable services of A. W. N. Pugin and John Thomas, and their share of the credit has been the subject of controversy. The building of the new Houses no doubt did much to advance a working knowledge of Gothic architecture by affording a training not only to draughtsmen but also to large numbers of craftsmen in several trades.

Meanwhile several younger men, whole-hearted Goths, were coming on. Three stand out a good deal ahead of the rest: George Gilbert Scott (1811–79), William Butterfield (1814–1900), and George Edmund Street (1824–81). Each of these owes a good deal to the influence of A. W. N. Pugin and of Benjamin Webb and his friends. Webb held the benefice of St. Andrew's, Wells Street, London, from 1862 till his death in 1885. He was the founder of the Cambridge Camden Society (afterwards the Ecclesiological Society) which did much to advance the Gothic Revival and the knowledge of ecclesiology.

During the thirty-three years 1845 to 1878 Scott built an extraordinary number of new churches and other buildings of steadily growing merit, for the most part in orthodox Gothic. St. John's College Chapel, Cambridge, in 1862, additions to New College, Oxford, Saint Mary Abbot's Church, Kensington, 1878, the great hall of Glasgow University and Edinburgh Cathedral may be taken as typical. His best-known works are the Saint Pancras Station and Hotel, London, and the Albert Memorial. The spanning of the station by one great roof was a fine conception; the pointed form of the arched trusses was suggested by the engineer, and it is unfortunate that Scott should have adopted it. In 1856 Scott submitted a Gothic design for a new Foreign Office, and thereupon there ensued a fierce and famous battle between Gothic and Classic, with Scott and Palmerston as generals. Scott eventually carried out the work, but he had to abandon his Gothic design.

William Butterfield's first important work was the College of Saint Augustine, Canterbury. In 1856 he built the chapel of Balliol College, Oxford, and in 1859 the church and adjoining buildings of All Saints', Margaret Street, London. This church was in several respects a new departure and had a good deal of influence. The brickwork is left exposed both inside and outside. Saint Albans, Holborn, and other churches followed and in 1868 the County Hospital at Winchester. Butterfield's most famous work was Keble College, Oxford, the chapel of which was completed in 1876 at a cost of £60,000. It has all Butterfield's qualities: his zeal, his freedom of thought, his largeness of idea and of handling; he has here indulged his love of colour with a considerable degree of success. Butterfield's work now commands the sympathy of architects. His colour theory, for which he struggled through life, 'seems to have been that such combinations were permissible as could be produced by uncoloured natural materials'. It was exactly because it was based on a theory that his colour failed. Unfortunately it obtained some degree of popularity, and to it we owe the mixture of red, yellow, and blue bricks between 1860 and 1880. At St. Cross near Winchester probably all the coloured decoration is based on remains of old paintings found in the church, but it is carried out in a mechanical way and with heavy earthy colours.

George Edmund Street was for some years an assistant to Scott. He made short tours in Italy and Spain, the results of which are occasionally apparent in his work. The early Gothic of France also had a decided influence upon him as on all architects of the medieval school at this time. Street soon secured a fair share of work and took rank with Scott as an ecclesiastical architect. He built, about 1856, the nave of Bristol Cathedral. In 1866 selected architects were invited to compete for the new Courts of Justice in the Strand which were to take the place of the old courts on the south side of Westminster Hall: a relic of the days when courts of justice were necessarily attached to the King's palace. Delay was caused by disputes over the merits of the plans sent in, and it was not till 1868 that Street was chosen, and the work begun. It was nearly, but not quite, finished at the time of his death in 1881. This great work has some very remarkable qualities and some very obvious defects. Broadly speaking, it may be said that the merits are due to the enthusiasm, the knowledge, and the artistic powers of the architect, and the faults to the ignorance and the parsimony of the First Commissioner of Works. The site was far too small, so that the buildings had to be crowded together, reducing what should have been large courtyards to tiny air shafts, thus dooming parts of the building to impenetrable darkness.

While the Gothic revival was thus making steady and rapid progress another group of architects was carrying on Classical architecture more or less on the old traditional lines. Some, as we have seen, strayed, like Wilkins at Cambridge, from the beaten track into flowery Tudor meads. Sir James Pennethorne (1801–71) was another of these. He built the Museum of Economic Geology between Piccadilly and Jermyn Street about 1852, and the University of London buildings in Burlington Gardens in 1866. His essay in Gothic is the Public Record Office (1852), a strong piece of work, coarse in detail and utterly unlike anything medieval. Barry, too, was Classical by temperament and training. While the Houses of Parliament were beginning he built the Reform Club in Pall Mall in 1837: an admirable building on the lines of an Italian palazzo.

Meanwhile the old guard of classical purists marched steadily on. Harvey Lonsdale Elmes (1813–47) built Saint George's Hall, Liverpool (1836), winning the first place in an open competition at the age of twenty-three. Sir Robert Smirke (1781–1867) had travelled in Greece when young. He built the British Museum in 1825–47, the east wing of Somerset House, and the central portion of the Customs House. The Reading Room of the

British Museum (1854–7) was the work of his brother
Sidney, who also built the Carlton Club and the Exhibition Galleries at Burlington House.

Decimus Burton built many town and country houses.
His most familiar work is the Park Entrance at Hyde
Park Corner (1825). George Basevi (1794–1845) had also
been a traveller. His greatest work is the Fitzwilliam
Museum at Cambridge (1837–45). Basevi was a cousin of
Lord Beaconsfield and his style has something of Jewish
opulence. Philip Hardwick (1792–1870) built the Gold-
smiths' Hall in 1829, but his better-known building is
Euston Station with its Greek Doric entrance portico
(1839); the Booking Hall is by his son. Sir William Tite
may be called the last of the old school. He was born in
1798, built the Royal Exchange between 1840 and 1844,
opposed the introduction of Gothic into Whitehall, and
did not die till 1873.

Charles Robert Cockerell (1788–1863) is the most
interesting figure of this group and perhaps of all the
architects of the nineteenth century. His work has rare
distinction and shows that new fields still remained to
be explored in Classical architecture. He was Greek in
his tastes and in his refinement, but he treated the style
with the freedom of a Roman, using arches and vaults.
While young he spent seven years in studying in Italy,
Sicily, Greece, and Asia Minor. He married the daughter
of John Rennie, the designer of Waterloo Bridge, but
this was eleven years after the completion of the bridge,
which, indeed, was built while he was abroad, so that he
can have had no hand in, or influence on, the work. His
chief works are: the Bristol Literary and Philosophical
Institution, 1822; the north wing of the Cambridge
University Library, 1837, a fragment only of a scheme
for rebuilding the whole of the Library; the Taylorian
Institution at Oxford, 1842; the offices of the Westminster Insurance Company in the Strand, London,
1832; the London and Westminster Bank in Lothbury,
1838, in conjunction with Sir John Soane.

14

The men whose work we have now noticed carry us three-quarters of the way through the nineteenth century. The fight they had fought for the Classic and Gothic styles was nearly over. For ecclesiastical buildings and colleges Gothic had carried all before it from the first. For public buildings Roman had more than held its own in spite of the triumphs of the Houses of Parliament and the Law Courts: the only two important buildings in which the style had been preserved consistently throughout. Neither style had advanced. Gothic at its best was hampered by medievalism and at its worst suffered from crass ignorance of the mere rudiments. Classic had rather slipped back from the point to which Sir William Chambers had carried it at Somerset House. The influence of original geniuses (like Butterfield and Cockerell) is slow to make itself felt. In Domestic architecture the towns still stuck to the old traditions but in the country, and especially in parsonage houses, Elizabethan or a meagre and acid Gothic had become common. Planning, which had at least since Roman times been a serious and noble art, had degenerated and had as yet given little promise of what it was to achieve in the future.

Orthodox Gothic was continued to the end of the century by several artists of distinction, who were but little junior to those who have been noticed above and belong to the same artistic generation. John Loughborough Pearson (1817–97), a fine architect, was a great church builder and restorer. His best-known works are Saint Augustine's, Kilburn (1870); Saint John's, Red Lion Square; Truro Cathedral (begun 1879), and the chancel added to the old Abbey Church at Shrewsbury.

George Frederick Bodley (1827–1907) was famous as a builder and decorator of refined and beautiful churches: Saint Michael's, Brighton; Hoar Cross Church (1870); churches at Clumber and Eccleston; church and buildings at Cowley; School Board Offices on the Thames Embankment. He worked from 1869 till 1898 in partnership with Thomas Garner (1839–1906), jointly on the same buildings till 1884 and after that separately on separate buildings. Bodley did much to lead Gothic architecture

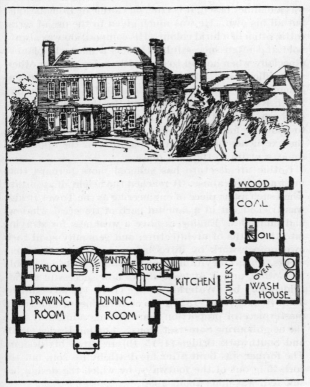

FIG. 179. EARLY NINETEENTH-CENTURY HOUSE

in the direction of simplicity and breadth, along which it was to be carried farther by later men. Garner designed the reredos of Saint Paul's Cathedral.

Alfred Waterhouse is typical of a totally different school. The men we have noticed produced buildings which might, but for their newness, be mistaken by the uninitiated for ancient work. Not so Waterhouse. His was a manner based, it is true, on Gothic or Romanesque, but all his own. He was much given to the use of terra-cotta, often of a lurid colour. His composition was always bold and often successful. He was a masterly planner especially when he had to deal with an irregular or other-wise difficult site. His best-known buildings are those at Manchester (1859–70); the Natural History Museum, South Kensington (1869–80); and the Prudential Offices, Holborn, finished in 1876. He was one of those invited to compete for the Law Courts, and was placed second, the excellence of his plan giving him, in the opinion of some, a claim to the first place.

Gothic architecture has suffered more perhaps than most arts from abuse. It reached the height of absurdity when such a fine piece of engineering as the Tower Bridge was tricked out in a fanciful garb of traceried windows and pinnacles. Engineers have a weakness for straying into the paths of architecture, and generally spoil their own proper work by introducing inconsequential orna-ments. It was inevitable that Westminster Bridge should be Gothic, and it at least shows how successful a wide bridge may be. Waterloo Bridge (1810–17) was built by John Rennie (1761–1821), the civil engineer. This was a masterpiece of proportion, harmonizing admirably with the neighbouring Somerset House. London Bridge (1831) and Southwark Bridge (1815–19) are from his designs. The former was built after his death by his son, but the corbelling out of the footways, by which the design has suffered, was done about 1900.

One contribution which the nineteenth century made to architecture was the development of the house plan. The larger eighteenth-century house left nothing to be desired in stately arrangement, but much in convenience. The medium-sized house had shown some development.

For the country 'cottage' there prevailed a stereotyped plan suitable only for the town: a narrow passage with a staircase along one side, a sitting-room on either hand, and some spacious but badly arranged kitchen offices in the rear or in a basement: a 'frontage' to the road, which

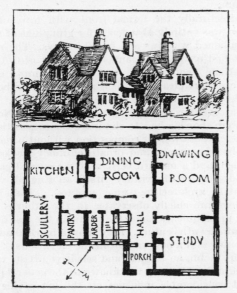

FIG. 180. LATE NINETEENTH-CENTURY HOUSE

was usually quite near, less important windows at the back, and blank side walls; all without regard to the points of the compass or the views to be had in various directions.

It was about the middle of the century, or rather earlier, that the break-away from this convention occurred. Possibly it was suggested by the additions which had been made to the old formal houses. Its development was probably due to several causes: the

desire for a view into the side garden, for a more picturesque staircase, and for a broken roof line. However that
may be there gradually developed a system of planning
of great variety which secured the best aspects and a
grouping of the rooms so as to reduce the service to a
minimum.

Architecturally the formal front with rows of sash
windows was entirely abandoned for groupings of gables
and mullioned windows and tall chimneys. The results
were at first a somewhat fantastic travesty of Gothic or
Elizabethan, though often the early attempts of the
forties are more pleasing in their picturesque exuberance
than the cold productions of twenty years later.

In the seventies and eighties Philip Webb and Norman
Shaw were showing how to eliminate the inessential and
produce effects by sheer composition without ornament.
Barge-boards, finials, and ornate chimney-stacks were
discarded, and a modern version of the curved gable of
the mid-seventeenth century—itself an English version
of Dutch architecture—was adopted. These later
tendencies are chiefly observable in the suburbs which
sprang up so quickly round the towns in the last quarter
of the nineteenth century. They show a marked advance
in planning and a new variant in the elevations.

Philip Webb, an original and sensitive artist, worked
in a free style. Not very well known to the general public,
he had considerable influence on the art of his time,
doing much by his example to expound the natural and
proper use of materials.

Richard Norman Shaw also exercised a great influence
on the architects of his day. He brought domestic
architecture back to the simpler forms of Queen Anne's
reign. His New Scotland Yard, a strong work, had at
the time a considerable effect on architecture. That
influence was not so durable as it might have been
because its creator was already moving on to fresh fields
and drawing others with him. In the new Piccadilly
Hotel and in the rebuilding of the Quadrant of Regent

Street he again broke new ground while using correct Classical models for his details.

Thomas Graham Jackson belonged to the same school as the earlier Shaw in his free use of Gothic, and of Jacobean with the casual introduction of Gothic features here and there. Hertford College Chapel, the Schools, and Brasenose at Oxford, the Law Library, with the Geological and other museums at Cambridge, and the Chapel of Giggleswick School may be cited as examples of his work.

The close of the century saw the beginning of a movement in the direction of simplicity in public buildings and in the larger commercial buildings. The influence of Sir William Chambers's Somerset House is observable. Mountford's Central Criminal Court (1907, on the site of the old Newgate Prison by Gandon), the buildings in Aldwych and its neighbourhood, the recent public offices in Whitehall, the London County Council Building and numerous business houses in the City and shops at the West End, form a remarkable output and show some unity of effort. Their most remarkable characteristic is the great increase in scale. Scale, in this connexion, refers not to the actual size of the building but to questions of treatment, such as number and size of the parts in relation to the whole. A comparison of Bush House or Selfridge's with the buildings of forty years ago will show what is meant. The weak point of all this city architecture is that its impressive monumental character is only skin deep. A few inches behind these stately columns and massive arches there is a framework of steel on which they depend for support. The system is defended on the ground of the economy of space effected by the use of small steel supports in place of massive brick piers. There now appears a disposition to question its durability. The smaller London houses, both in business parts such as the Strand and in the West End, passed through a phase, curiously miscalled Queen Anne, characterized by complex and fanciful Dutch and German detail.

This was chiefly between 1880 and 1890. After that they began to follow the simpler treatment of the true Queen Anne of Kensington Palace.

In ecclesiastical architecture Gothic still held the field. J. D. Sedding, R. J. Johnson, and Temple Moore continued the old traditions. But towards the end of the century Byzantine architecture was popularized by the great success, so far at least as the interior is concerned, of Westminster Cathedral (1895), by John Francis Bentley (1839–1902).

The architecture of the nineteenth century was culled from every city between Constantinople and Dublin. Starting in complete ignorance of the medieval art, even of our own country, it closed with at least a bowing acquaintance with not only the national, but with a dozen other styles. This necessarily involved in destruction the whole body of traditional lore in building craft. It is probably responsible too for the destruction of what little was left of that instinctive sense of design which even the ordinary builder seems to have possessed and to have preserved from old time for the first generation of the nineteenth century. The builder lost his tradition, but was, of course, quite unable to keep pace with the new learning. Hence speculative building, forming as it did such an enormous proportion of the total output, gradually descended to the deepest bathos.

Architecture has not commonly been a popular art. The middle age of Europe was abnormal in creating an architecture of the people, for the people, and by the people. Generally, in a greater or less degree, it has been a 'mystery' practised by the few. Such, emphatically, is must be now. And as such, though dead as a popular tradition, it shows plenty of vitality.

NOTE

IN making the following list of buildings, the aim has been
to select examples which are at once typical, easily accessible,
and widely distributed. The dates to which Saxon buildings
are assigned are those proposed by Mr. Micklethwaite. For
those of the medieval period I am chiefly indebted to Mr.
Parker's edition of 'Rickman,' and for most buildings after
1500 to Mr. Blomfield's *Renaissance Architecture of England*.
The dates assigned to the buildings, and to the births and
deaths of the architects, are approximate only, for authorities
disagree even in regard to those of recent times. The grouping
and the marginal notes, for which I am myself responsible,
are, of course, arbitrary, and are meant to indicate only
general tendencies, but they will be perhaps not more misleading than the usual division into styles.

In the table of Religious Orders, the date at which each
was introduced into England and the number of houses
suppressed are, in most cases, taken from Dr. Gasquet's
English Monastic Life.

II.—CHRONOLOGICAL LIST
OF BUILDINGS AND ARCHITECTS

ROMANO-BRITISH.
- Wall of Hadrian, Carlisle to Newcastle; A.D. 120.
- Silchester, Berkshire, foundations of town and Christian church (buried); probably about A.D. 350.
- Other Roman towns, villas, etc.; 3rd and 4th centuries.
- British Buildings continuing the Roman methods; first half of the 5th century.

*
- Canterbury, St. Martin's Church, chancel; before 600.
- Canterbury, St. Pancras' Church; before 600.

CELTIC.
- Monkwearmouth Church, Durham; A.D. 674.
- Escomb Church, Durham; late 7th century.
- Jarrow Church, Durham (not the tower); late 7th century.
- Bradford-on-Avon Church, Wiltshire; c. 700.
- Barton-on-the-Humber, Lincolnshire, tower.

TRANSITION.
- Dover, St. Mary's Church, in the Castle; 7th century.
- Repton Church, Derbyshire, crypt; 7th century.
- Britford Church, Wiltshire, arches in nave; 9th century.
- Worth, Sussex, part of church; 11th century.

BASILICAN.
- Hexham Church, Northumberland, crypt; probably c. 670.
- Ripon Minster, Yorkshire, crypt; probably c. 670.
- Wing, Buckinghamshire, church with crypt; c. 680.
- Brixworth, Northants, church with crypt; c. 680.

ENGLISH.
- Deerhurst, Gloucestershire, St. Mary's Church; tower early, east end 11th century.
- Lincoln, St. Peter at Gowt's Church; 10th or 11th century.
- Lincoln, St. Mary le Wigford Church; 10th or 11th century.
- Earl's Barton Church, Northants, tower; 10th or 11th century.
- Sompting Church, Sussex, tower; 11th century.
- Cambridge, St. Benedict's Church, tower; 11th century.

* Roman tradition (Micklethwaite)

Tower of London, The White Tower; about 1070–1138.

St. Albans Abbey Church; 1077–93.

Winchester Cathedral, crypt and transepts; 1079–93.

Ely Cathedral, transepts and east part of nave; 1083–1100.

Durham Cathedral, choir and transepts; 1093–6.

Norwich Cathedral, choir, transepts and nave; 1096–1119.

Tewkesbury Abbey Church, west front and nave arches; 1103–21.

Durham Cathedral, nave and aisles; 1104–33.

Peterborough Cathedral; 1117–43.

London, St. Bartholomew's Church, Smithfield; 1132–33.

Cambridge, Holy Sepulchre Church; probably c. 1125.

Rochester Castle; 1126–38.

Fountains Abbey, Yorks, nave and transepts, 1132–47.

Buildwas, Shropshire, Abbey Church, nave; 1135–60.

St. Cross, Winchester, hospital, choir of church; 1136–.

Oxford Cathedral, 1160–80.

Iffley Church, Oxfordshire, nave, west front, and tower; 1160–.

Oakham, Rutland, castle; 1165–91.

Ely Cathedral, west transepts and tower; 1174–89.

Canterbury Cathedral, choir; 1175–84.

Durham Cathedral, galilee; 1180–97.

Glastonbury Abbey, St. Joseph's Chapel; 1185–1200.

London, Temple Church, round part; –1185.

Lincoln Cathedral, choir (not presbytery), north transept and part of south; 1192–1200.

Winchester Cathedral, presbytery and Lady Chapel; 1195–1204.

Worcester Cathedral, choir; 1203–18.

Salisbury Cathedral; 1220–58.

Winchester, King's Hall; 1222–35.

Exeter Cathedral, chapter house; 1224–44.

Wells Cathedral, nave and west front; 1225–39.

Rochester Cathedral, part of choir; 1225 (transepts, central tower, and east bays of nave rather later.)

York Minster, south transept; 1227–40.

Southwell Minster, choir; 1233–94.

Ely Cathedral, presbytery; 1235–52.

Peterborough Cathedral, west front; 1237–.

Netley Abbey, Hampshire; 1239–.

Durham Cathedral, Chapel of the Nine Altars; 1242–90.

Westminster Abbey, choir and transepts; 1245–69.

MONASTERIES, CASTLES, AND CHURCHES.

CATHEDRALS.

Wells Cathedral, Lady Chapel; 1248-64.
Lincoln Cathedral, presbytery; 1260-80.
Salisbury Cathedral, cloister and chapter-house; 1263-84.
Oxford, Merton College Chapel, choir: 1274.
Wells Cathedral, chapter house; 1292-1302.
Stokesay, Salop, castle; 1291-.
York Cathedral, nave; 1291-1345.
St. Albans Abbey Church, Lady Chapel; 1308-26.
Lichfield Cathedral, Lady Chapel; 1310-21.
Bristol Cathedral, choir; 1311.
Gloucester Cathedral, south aisle of nave; 1318-29.
Lichfield Cathedral, west front; 1320.
Ely Cathedral, Lady Chapel and octagon; 1321-49.
Bury St. Edmunds, gateway of abbey; 1327-.
Exeter Cathedral, nave; 1331-50.
York Minster, west window; 1338.
Penshurst, Kent, hall; 1341-.
Norborough, Northamptonshire, hall; 1356-.
Hull, Holy Trinity Church; -1367.
Selby Abbey, Yorkshire, choir; -1375.
Canterbury Cathedral, nave and west transepts; 1378-1411.

PARISH CHURCHES, COLLEGES, HOUSES, AND GUILD HALLS.

Oxford, New College; 1380-86.
York Cathedral, central tower; 1389-1407.
Exeter Cathedral, east window; 1390-2.
Winchester Cathedral, nave and aisles remodelled; 1394-1410.
Westminster Hall, roof and porch, etc.; 1397-9.
Coventry, St. Mary's Hall; 1401-14.
Howden Church, Yorkshire; 1403-.
York Minster, east window; 1405-8.
Norwich, Guildhall; 1413.
Gloucester Cathedral, west front and south porch; 1420-37.
Manchester Cathedral; 1422-.
Oxford, Merton College, transepts; -1424.
Tattershall Castle, Lincolnshire; 1433-55.
South Wingfield Manor House, Derbyshire; 1433-55.
Fotheringhay Church, Northamptonshire; 1435.
Warkworth Castle; 1435-40.
Oxford, Divinity School; 1445-54.
Oxford, Merton College, tower; 1448-50.
Gloucester Cathedral, central tower; 1454-57.
Long Melford Church; chiefly c. 1470 and 1496.
Norwich Cathedral, clearstory and choir vault; 1472-99.

THE END OF GOTHIC.

Windsor, St. George's Chapel, except vault; 1481–1508.
Canterbury Cathedral, central tower; 1490–1517.
Oxford, Magdalen College, tower; 1492–1505.
Bath, Abbey Church; 1500–39.
Windsor, St. George's Chapel, vault; 1507–20.
Cambridge, King's College Chapel, turrets, pinnacles, large windows and vault; 1508–15.
Thornbury Castle, Gloucestershire (unfinished); 1511–.
Westminster, Henry VII's Chapel; 1503–20.

GOTHIC WITH RENAISSANCE DETAILS. BY ITALIANS.

Westminster, Tomb of Henry VII, by Torrigiano; 1512.
Hampton Court; 1515–20.
Layer Marney Gall, Essex (ruinous); about 1520.
Sutton Place, Surrey; 1521–7.
Compton Winyate House, Warwickshire; about 1520.
Hengrave Hall, Suffolk; 1525–38.
Oxford, Christ Church Hall; –1529.
Ely Cathedral, Chantry Chapel of Bishop West; 1525–33.

BY GERMANS.

Burghley House, Northamptonshire; about 1556.
Charlcote House, Warwickshire; about 1558.
Longleat, Wiltshire; 1567–80.
Montacute House; 1580–1601.
Knole House, Kent (parts).
Blickling, Norfolk.

GREAT COUNTRY HOUSES. BY SURVEYORS AND ARCHITECT-BUILDERS.

John Thorpe, fl. 1570–*c.* 1610, surveyor.
Longford Castle, Wiltshire; 1580–*c.* 1590.
Rushton Hall, Northamptonshire; 1595–1630.

Huntingdon Smithson, died 1648, surveyor.
Wollaton Hall, Nottinghamshire; 1580–.
Bolsover Castle, Derbyshire; 1613–*c.* 1630.

Thomas Holt, 1578?–1624, carpenter.
Oxford, The Schools; 1600.

Ralph Symons, builder; *fl.* 1600.
Cambridge, St. John's College (second court); 1598–1602.
Cambridge, Trinity College Hall; 1604.

John Westley, died 1656, bricklayer, and *Thomas Grumbald,* mason.
Cambridge, Clare College, east and south ranges and bridge, 1638–41.

John Abel, 1597–1694, carpenter.
Leominster, Hereford, Market Hall ('The Grange').
Abbey Dore Church, Hereford, woodwork.

BUILDINGS BY ARCHITECTS.

> *Inigo Jones*, 1573–1652.
>
> Greenwich Hospital, Queen's House; 1617–35.
> London, Banqueting House, Whitehall Palace; 1619–22.
> Raynham Park, Norfolk; 1636.
> London, Lindsay House, Lincoln's Inn Fields; 1640.
> London, St. Paul's Church, Covent Garden (since destroyed, but rebuilt on the old lines).
> Wilton House, Wiltshire, south block; 1649.
>
> *John Webb*, 1611–74.
>
> Thorpe Hall, Northamptonshire; 1656.
> London, Houses in Great Queen Street.
> Ramsbury House, Wiltshire.
> Ashdown Park, Berkshire; probably *c.* 1665.

SURVIVAL OF GOTHIC.

> Oxford, Wadham College; 1610–13.
> Bath Abbey Church, continued till 1616.
> Cambridge, St. John's College Library; 1624.
> London, St. Catherine Cree Church; 1630.
> Lytes Cary Hall, Somerset; 1631.
> Cambridge, Peterhouse Chapel; 1632.
> Leeds, St. John's Church; 1633.
> Berwick-on-Tweed Church; 1648–52.
> Plymouth, Charles Church; 1657.
> Oxford, Brasenose College Chapel; –1666.

RENAISSANCE POPULARIZED.

> *Sir Christopher Wren*, 1632–1723.
>
> Oxford, Sheldonian Theatre; 1663.
> Cambridge, Trinity College Library; 1675–90.
> London, fifty-three City churches; 1670–1711.
> London, St. Paul's Cathedral; 1675–1717.
> Hampton Court; 1698–1700.
> Greenwich Hospital.
>
> *No architect.*
>
> Nottingham Castle; *c.* 1675–.
>
> *Henry Bell*, died 1717, of King's Lynn.
>
> King's Lynn, Norfolk, Customs House; 1681.
> North Runction Church, Norfolk; 1718.
>
> *William Talman*, died 1700.
>
> Chatsworth House, Derbyshire; 1681.

AMATEURISM.

Henry Aldrich, Dean of Christchurch, Oxford, 1647–1710, amateur.
Oxford, All Saints' Church; *c.* 1695.
Oxford, Peckwater quadrangle, Christ Church; *c.* 1695.

George Clarke, statesman (Secretary for War, etc.), 1660–1736, amateur.
Oxford, Christ Church Library; 1716.

Sir John Vanbrugh, 1664–1726; amateur or professional?
Castle Howard, Yorkshire; 1701–14.
Blenheim Palace, Oxfordshire; 1705–24.

Nicholas Hawksmoor, 1666–1736.
London, St. Mary Woolnoth Church; 1716–19.
London, St. George's Church, Bloomsbury; 1720.

INFLUENCE OF WREN.

Thomas Archer, died 1743.
Birmingham, St. Philip's Church; 1710.

James Gibbs, 1682–1754.
London, St. Mary le Strand Church; 1714–17.
London, St. Martin-in-the-Fields Church; 1721–6.
Cambridge, Senate House; 1722.
Oxford, Radcliffe Library; 1734–47.
Ditchley House, Oxfordshire.

COPIES OF ITALIAN BUILDINGS.

Giacomo Leoni, 1686–1746 (came to England *c.* 1715).
Moor Park, Hertfordshire; 1720.

Colin Campbell, died 1734.
Mereworth Castle, Kent; about 1720.
Houghton House, Norfolk; 1723.

Thomas Ripley, died 1758.
London, Admiralty Offices; 1724–26 (screen by Adams).

Earl of Burlington (Richard Boyle, third earl), 1695–1753, amateur. Credited with:
Works perhaps by Campbell, Kent, Leoni, Flitcroft.

Sir James Borough, Master of Gonville and Caius College, Cambridge, 1690–1764, amateur, worked with James Essex, architect.
Cambridge, Work at Peterhouse, etc.; 1732.
Cambridge, Clare College Chapel; 1763–9.

William Kent, 1684–1748.
London Horse Guards; 1742.
Holkham Hall, Norfolk; about 1744.

Henry Flitcroft, 1697–1769.
London, St. Giles'-in-the-Fields Church; 1731.
Wentworth House, Yorkshire; 1740.
Woburn Abbey, Bedfordshire; 1747.

George Dance, senior, 1698–1768.
London, Mansion House; 1739.

Isaac Ware, died, 1766.
London, Chesterfield House; 1749.

John Wood, senior, 1705 (?)–1754, of Bath.
Prior Park, near Bath; *c.* 1750.
Bath, Queen's Square (north side), etc.
Bristol, Exchange.
Liverpool, Exchange; –1754.

Stephen Wright.
Cambridge, University Library, east front; 1755–8.

John Vardy, died 1765.
London, Spencer House; 1762.

James Stuart, 1713–88.
No. 15 St. James's Square.
Published 'Antiquities of Athens', 1763.

Sir Robert Taylor, 1714–88.
London, Stone Buildings, Lincoln's Inn Fields.

James Paine, c. 1720–89.
Kedleston Hall, Derbyshire; 1761.
Worksop Hall, Nottinghamshire; 1763.
Thorndon Hall, Essex; 1763.

Nicholas Revett, 1720–1804.
Chapel at Ayot, St. Lawrence, Herts.
Published, with J. Stuart, 'Antiquities of Athens'.

John Carr, 1723–1807, of York.
Harewood House, Yorkshire; 1760 (since altered).
Basildon Park, Berkshire; 1776.

Sir William Chambers, 1726–96.
London, Somerset House; 1775.

GREEK INFLUENCE.

Robert Adam, 1728–92.
London, Lansdowne House; 1765.
Luton House, Bedfordshire; 1767.

George Dance, junior, 1741–1825.
London, St. Luke's Hospital, Old Street.

Henry Edward Goodridge, 1797–1865.
Bath, Lansdown Tower, 1825.

James Gandon, 1742–1823.
Dublin Customs House; 1781.

Henry Holland, 1746 (?)–1806.
London, Brook's Club; 1777.

James Wyatt, 1746–1813.
Heaton House, near Manchester; 1772 (Greco-Italian).
Fonthill Abbey, Wilts; 1795 (Gothic).
Nave of Hereford Cathedral; 1786 (Gothic).
London, Front of White's Club.

John Nash, 1752–1835.
London, Regent Street, Portland Place, etc.; 1813–20.
London, Marble Arch (Greco-Roman).

Sir John Soane, 1753–1837.
London, Bank of England; 1788.

John Rennie, 1761–1821. (Engineer).
London, Waterloo Bridge; 1810–17 (Greco-Roman).

EARLY GOTHIC REVIVAL.

Augustus Charles Pugin, 1762–1832.
Published 'Examples of Gothic Architecture . . . in
    England,' 1831.

Sir Jeffry Wyatville (formerly Jeffry Wyatt), 1766–
    1840.
Cambridge, Sidney-Sussex College; 1824–30 (Eliza-
    bethan).
Windsor Castle; 1824–30 (Gothic).

William Inwood, 1771(?)–1843.
London, St. Pancras Church, Marylebone Road; 1819–
    22 (Greek).

Thomas Rickman, 1776–1841.
Birmingham, St. George's Church, 1819.
Cambridge, New Court, St. John's College; 1831.
Published 'An Attempt to discriminate the Different
    Styles of Architecture in England from the Con-
    quest to the Reformation,' 1817.

15

GREEK AND GRECO-ROMAN.

William Wilkins, 1778–1839.
Cambridge, Downing College, 1807–11 (Greek).
The Grange, Hampshire, 1809 (Greek).
Dalmeny House, 1814–17 (Gothic).
Cambridge, Hall, etc., King's College, 1822 (Gothic).
London, University College, 1828 (Greek).
London, National Gallery, 1832–8 (Greek).

Thomas Hamilton, 1784–1858.
Edinburgh, College of Physicians. High School, 1825.

Sir Robert Smirke, 1781–1867.
London, British Museum, 1823–47. (Reading Room
    by his brother Sidney, 1854–7.)
London, East Wing, Somerset House 1828–31.
London, College of Physicians, 1825.

Francis Goodwin, 1784–1835.
Manchester, Old Town Hall, 1822–4.

Edward Blore, 1787–1879.
London, Restored and part rebuilt Lambeth Palace.
Cambridge, Pitt Press.
Abbotsford, 1816.   (All Gothic.)

Charles Robert Cockerell, 1788–1863.
Cambridge, University Library, 1837.
Oxford, Taylor Institute, 1842.

Lewis Vulliamy, 1791–1871.
London, Dorchester House, 1848–57.

Thomas Hardwick, 1752–1829
London, Marylebone Parish Church (Greek) 1813–17.

Philip Hardwick, 1792–1870.
London, Hall of Goldsmith's Company, 1829, Euston
    Station.

George Stanley Repton, died 1858.
London, St. Philip's Chapel, Regent Street (Greek).
    Destroyed 1906.

George Basevi, 1794–1845.
London, Houses in Belgrave Square.
Cambridge, Fitzwilliam Museum, 1837–45 (Roman).

Sir Charles Barry, 1795–1860.
London, Traveller's Club, 1829.
Birmingham, Edward VI's School, 1833.
Manchester, Athenæum, 1836.
London, Reform Club, 1837 (Italian Renaissance).
London, Houses of Parliament, 1849–60 (Gothic).

Sir William Tite, 1798–1873.
London, Royal Exchange, 1840–4.

Decimus Burton, 1800–81.
London, Park Entrance at Hyde Park Corner, 1825 (Roman).

Sir James Pennethorne, 1801–71.
London, Museum of Geology; *c.* 1852 (Italian Renaissance).
London, Record Office; *c.* 1852 (Gothic).
Somerset House, West Wing, 1852–6 (Roman).
London University, Burlington Gardens, 1866.

David Bryce, 1803–76.
Edinburgh, British Linen Company's Bank, 1850.

Thomas Henry Wyatt, 1807–80.
London, Cavalry Barracks, Knightsbridge.

James Fergusson, 1808–86.
Published 'History of Architecture', 1855–76.

Sir George Gilbert Scott, 1811–78.
London, Foreign Office, 1861.
London, Albert Memorial, 1864.
London, St. Pancras Station and Hotel, 1865.
London, Home and Colonial Office, 1870.
Cambridge, Chapel of St. John's College, 1863.
London, St. Mary Abbot's Church, Kensington, 1878.

Augustus Welby Northmore Pugin, 1812–52 (son of A. C. Pugin).
Assisted Sir C. Barry with designs for Houses of Parliament.
Built many new buildings.
Published 'Contrast's, 1836; 'True Principles', 1842; 'Apology', 1843.

Harvey Lonsdale Elmes, 1813–47.
Liverpool, St. George's Hall, 1836.

William Butterfield, 1814–1900.
Oxford, Chapel, Balliol College, 1856.
London, All Saints' Church, Margaret Street, 1859.
London, St. Alban's Church, Holborn, 1863.
Winchester, County Hospital, 1868.
Oxford, Keble College, 1876.
Cathedrals at Melbourne, Adelaide, Bombay, Poona,
    Cape Town, Port Elizabeth, Madagascar.

Benjamin Woodward, 1815–61.
Oxford, Museum, 1855–68.

John Loughborough Pearson, 1817–97.
London, St. Augustine's Church, Kilburn; *c.* 1870.
London, St. John's Church, Red Lion Square.
Truro Cathedral, 1879.
Cambridge, Sidney-Sussex College and University
    Library.

Francis Fowke, Captain, R.E., 1823–65.
London, South Kensington Museum Galleries.
London, Albert Hall, main features, *c.* 1865.

George Edmund Street, 1824–81.
London, Law Courts, 1868–82.
Bristol, Nave of Cathedral.

George Frederick Bodley, 1827–1907.
Hoar Cross Church; *c.* 1870.
St. Augustine's Church, Pendlebury, 1874.
Churches at Clumber, Eccleston, and Cowley.
Oxford, Buildings at Magdalen College, Christ Church,
    and University College,
Cambridge, King's and Queen's Colleges.
London, School Board Offices.

William Burges, 1827–81.
Oxford, Hall of Worcester College.
Cork Cathedral.
London, His own house, Melbury Road, Kensington.

Thomas Garner, 1830–1906.
Churches at Bedworth, Peasdown, and Camerton.
London, Reredos in St. Paul's Cathedral, 1888.

Alfred Waterhouse, 1830–1905.
Manchester, Assize Courts, 1859; Owen's College, 1870 and Town Hall, 1877.
London, Natural History Museum, 1868–80.
London, Prudential Assurance Offices, Holborn.

Edward Middleton Barry, 1831–80.
London, Charing Cross Hotel.

Philip Webb, 1831–1915.
Clouds, near Salisbury, 1880.
Red House, Bexley Heath, 1859.
London, House on the Green, Kensington Palace Gardens, 1868.

Richard Norman Shaw, 1831–1912.
London, Church of St. Michael and All Angels, Bedford Park.
London, New Scotland Yard, 1890–2, 1907.
London, Quadrant of Regent Street and Piccadilly Hotel.

Sir Thomas Graham Jackson, 1835–1920.
Oxford, Schools, etc.
Cambridge, Law Library, etc.
Wrote on Byzantine, Romanesque, and Gothic, 1913, 1915.

John Dando Sedding, 1938–91.
Bournemouth, Church and Vicarage of St. Clement.
Falmouth, All Saints' Church.
London, Church of the Holy Redeemer, Clerkenwell.
London, Church of the Holy Trinity, Chelsea.

George Gilbert Scott, the younger, 1839–97. *s.* of Sir G. G. Scott.
Norwich, Roman Catholic Church.

John Francis Bentley, 1839–1910.
London, Roman Catholic Cathedral, 1894–1910.

John Belcher, 1841–1913.
London, Institute of Chartered Accountants, 1889.
Colchester, Town Hall, 1897.
London, Church of the Holy Trinity, Kingsway.

Edward William Mountford, 1855–1908.
Sheffield, Town Hall, 1890.
Liverpool, Museum and Technical School.
London, Town Hall, etc., Battersea.
London, Central Criminal Court, 1907.

REVIVAL OF SECULAR ARCHITECTURE.

III.—TABLE OF THE
PERIODS OF ENGLISH ARCHITECTURE

		Rickman.	Sharpe.
			Saxon to 1066
William I	1066	Norman	Norman
William II	1087	1066–1189	1066–1145
Henry I	1100		
Stephen	1135		
Henry II	1154		Transition 1145–1190
Richard I	1189	Early English	Lancet
John	1199	1189–1280	1190–1245
Henry III	1216		
Edward I	1272	Decorated	Geometrical
Edward II	1307	1280–1377	1245–1315
Edward III	1327		Curvilinear 1315–1360
Richard II	1377	Perpendicular	Perpendicular
Henry IV	1399	1377–1547	1360–1550
Henry V	1413		
Henry VI	1422		
Edward IV	1461		
Edward V	1483		
Richard III	1483		
Henry VII	1485		
Henry VIII	1509	Tudor *or* Elizabethan 1550–1603	
Edward VI	1547		
Mary	1553		
Elizabeth	1558		
James I	1603	Stuart *or* Jacobean 1603–1689	
Charles I	1625		
Commonwealth	1649		
Charles II	1661		
James II	1685		
William and Mary	1689	Hanoverian *or* Queen Ann 1689–1763	
Anne	1702		
George I	1714		
George II	1727		
George III	1760	Greek Revival, 1763–1820	
George IV	1820	Gothic Revival, 1820–1880	
William IV	1830		
Victoria	1837		
Edward VII	1900	Revival of Secular Arch^re 1880	
George V	1910		

IV.—A TABLE OF THE RELIGIOUS ORDERS IN ENGLAND AT THE TIME OF THE GENERAL SUPPRESSION BY HENRY VIII.

	Common name.	Founder.	When founded.	Rule, Habit, etc. When introduced into England.	No. of houses suppressed.
MONKS AND NUNS:					
Benedictine .	Black monks.	St. Benedict, at Monte Cassino, between Rome and Naples.	529	Black cape and hood over cassock of black, white, or russet, with white or black fur.	287
Cluniac .	..	Berno, at Cluny.	910	Reformed Benedictines. All black. 1077.	32
Carthusian .	..	St. Bruno, of Cologne, at Chartreuse, near Grenoble	1086	No houses of women in England. Black cloak, white tunic. 1181.	
Cistercian .	White monks or Grey monks.	Robert, Bishop of Molême, and St. Stephen Harding, at Citeaux, Dijon.	1098	Reformed Benedictines. White cassock with small hood, with black scapulary. 1128.	100
Fontevraud .	..	Robert d'Arbrissel at Fontevraud, Poitiers.	c. 1100	Double houses for men and women, ruled by Abbess. (No nuns in England?) 1161.	3
CANONS AND CANONESSES:					
Augustinian, incl. Trinitarians .	Black canons.	Probably at Avignon.	c. 1100	Black cloak and hood over white tunic. c. 1100.	170
Praemonstratensian	White canons.	St. Norbert, at Prémontré, Picardy.	1120	Reformed Augustinians. Long white cloak and hood over white cassock; white cap. 1140.	34

201

Gilbertine	..	St. Gilbert of Sempringham, at Sempringham, Lincolnshire.	1148	The only English order. Double houses for men and women, ruled by Abbess. Men, white cloak over black cassock; women, black cloak, hood, and tunic.	26
FRIARS AND NUNS:					
Franciscan	Grey friars or Friars minors.	St. Francis, at Assisi.	1208	Grey cloak and hood, grey cassock. 1224.	66
Dominican	Black friars or Preaching friars.	St. Dominic, at Bologna.	1215	Black cloak and hood over white tunic, square black cap. 1221.	58
Augustinian, including Crutched or Crossed	Austen Friars.	Not known.	13th cent.	No houses of women in England. Long black gown, with wide sleeves and hood; white cassock. 1250.	38
Carmelite	White Friars.	Albert of Jerusalem, at Mount Carmel.	1209?	White cloak over brown tunic. 1240.	40
St. Clare	Poor Clares or Minoresses.	St. Francis and St. Clara, at Assisi.	1212	Franciscan nuns. 1293. [1257.	3
Bonhommes	..	..	c. 1250	Rule of St. Augustine. Blue.	2
Brigittine	Order of Our Saviour.	St. Bridget of Sweden, at Wadstena.	c. 1350	Rule of St. Augustine. Black. 1414	1
MILITARY ORDERS:					
Hospitallers	..	Gerard, at Jerusalem.	1104	Black mantle, with eight-pointed white cross. 1100.	54
[Templars]	..	Hugh de Payens, at Jerusalem.	1118	White mantle with red cross; dark clothes; hair worn short. c. 1140. Supp. 1310.	23

GLOSSARY

Abacus. The top member of a capital.

FIG. 181
ABACI

FIG. 182
THE ROMAN ACANTHUS

Acanthus. The leaf of the Corinthian capital.

Almonry. A building where alms were distributed.

Altar, Portable-, or **Super-.** A small slab, about 12 inches by 6 inches, for use where there was no fixed altar. Allowed only by licence of the Pope. The term super-altar is now applied to the shelf at the back of the communion-table.

Altar-tomb. A tomb resembling a stone altar.

Ambo, Ambone. A pulpit-like lectern in early churches from which the gospel was read; there was a separate one for the epistle.

Ambulatory. A passage; the term is applied to cloisters, and to the aisle round an apse, etc.

Andirons. Fire dogs.

Annulet. A ring; the term is applied to the fillets under the Doric capital, and to the bands connecting small detached shafts with the central column or with the wall in Gothic. (Fig. 30.)

Anta. A short wall projecting from a building enclosing the end of a portico, or a pilaster in place of the wall where the portico is open. [Classic.]

Arabesque. A fanciful scroll ornament of leaves and animals and human beings. (Fig. 97.) [Renaissance.]

Architrave. The lowest and weight-carrying division of the entablature; the moulding round a door or window. [Classic and Renaissance.]

Ashlar. Squared and regular masonry.

Atrium. The central and partly covered court of a Roman house.

Attic. A storey above the main entablature.

Aumbry. A small cupboard in a wall.

FIG. 183
ARCHITRAVE
MOULDING

Baldachino (pron. baldakēno). A canopy; the term is generally applied to an altar canopy.

Ball-flower. (Fig. 59.)

Barge-board. A board placed under the gable when the roof projects beyond the wall.

Barrel vault. A vault like a railway tunnel.

Basilica. (p. 85.)

Batter. When a wall is intentionally built with a sloping face it is said 'to batter'.

Bay. A compartment of a building; the space between two pairs of columns or two roof principals.

Bay-window. A bow-window.

Bead. A small round moulding. (Fig. 183.)

Bed-mould. The moulding under the bold projection of a cornice.

Bevel. A slope made by cutting off an angle.

Bilection-mould. See **Bolection-mould.**

Billet. A Norman enrichment consisting of a succession of short cylinders lying in a shallow hollow or on a chamfer. (Fig. 31.)

Blind storey. A triforium.

Blocking-course. A plain course of stone over a cornice; a plain string-course. [Classic and Ren.] (Fig. 102.)

Bolection-mould. A moulding used in wood panelling, projecting beyond the face of the framing. [Ren.]

FIG. 184. BOLECTION-MOULD

Bond. The overlapping of stones or bricks in a wall.
In brickwork from the middle of the sixteenth
century to the end of the seventeenth century
English bond was used. In this system, which is the
strongest, one course consists entirely of headers,
i.e. bricks showing their ends, and the next course
of 'stretchers', or bricks showing their sides, and
so on alternately. In *Flemish bond* all courses are
alike, and show alternately 'headers' and stretchers'.

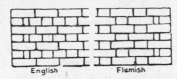

English   Flemish

FIG. 185
ENGLISH AND FLEMISH BOND

Bowtel. A round moulding. [Gothic.]

FIG. 186
BOWTEL
MOULDING,
WITH FILLET AT *a*.

(*a*)   (*b*)

FIG. 187
(*a*) A STONE BROACH SPIRE;
(*b*) TIMBER SPIRE COVERED
WITH SHINGLES.

Brace. A strut to connect two pieces of timber which are at right angles to one another.

Brattishing. (Fig. 86.)

Broach. A half pyramid connecting the angle of a square tower with the face of an octagonal spire. (Fig. 187 a.)

Cabled flute. See **Flute.**

Camber. An upward curve or slope in a beam, such as the tie-beam of a roof. (Fig. 49.)

Cantilever. A bracket.

Carrell. (p. 126.)

Caryatides. Columns in the form of human or grotesque figures.

Casement. (1) A wide, shallow moulding (Fig. 81); (2) a window hinged at the side to open like a door.

Chamfer. A bevel.

Checker. The office of an accountant in the Middle Ages.

Chevron. (Fig. 24.)

Clearstory, or Clerestory. The storey of the nave which is above the roofs of the aisles.

Coffer. A sunk panel in a ceiling, dome, or vault in Classic or Renaissance buildings.

Common-house. (p. 128.)

Composite order. (p. 66.)

Console. A bracket supporting the cornice over a doorway or window. [Classic] (Fig. 119.)

Corinthian order. (p. 66.)

Crenelle. A parapet with battlements or loopholes.

Crocket. A crook-like leaf or bunch of leaves projecting from the slope of a gable.

Cusp. One of a series of points projecting from the soffit or mouldings of an arch, giving a trefoil or multifoil form to the arch.

FIG. 188.
CUSP

Decastyle. A portico with a row of ten columns is said to be Decastyle. [Classic]

Dentil. An enrichment in a classical cornice consisting of a series of small square projections.

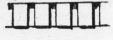

FIG. 189
DENTIL ENRICHMENT

Diaper. A geometrical pattern carved or painted on a wall in the Middle Ages.

Dog-tooth. (Fig. 46.)

Doric order. (p. 64.)

Dormer window. A window in a roof.

Dorsal. A curtain at the back of an altar.

Egg and dart. An enrichment in a classical cornice consisting alternately of eggs and darts.

FIG. 190
EGG-AND-DART
ENRICHMENT

Elemosinaria. An almonry (*see above*).

Enrichment. A small repeating ornament carved on a moulding, e.g. ball-flower, battlement, dentil, dog-tooth, egg-and-dart, zigzag.

Entablature. The horizontal superstructure on the columns in classical architecture. It is divided into three parts: the architrave or lintel, the frieze, and the cornice or projecting member.

Entasis. The slight swelling in a column. [Classic.]

Faldstool. A folding stool, formerly used for carrying about. The term is now applied to the Litany desk.

Fillet. A band; applied principally to mouldings. (Fig. 186.)

Flute. One of a series of channels running up the face of a column. Sometimes it is filled by a staff, which runs up to one-third of the height of the column, and it is then said to be cabled or reeded. [Classic and Ren.]

Footpace. A low platform, a dais.

Frater. The dining-hall in a monastery.

Freestone. Stone which can be worked with the chisel.

Frieze. The middle division of an entablature.

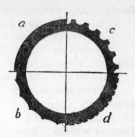

FIG. 191

QUARTER-PLANS OF COLUMNS:

(*a*) PLAIN SHAFT; (*b*) DORIC FLUTES; (*c*) IONIC AND CIRINTHIAN FLUTES; (*d*) CABLED FLUTES

Galilee. The term is applied to a porch, as at Lincoln, and to a chapel, as at Durham, and seems to have been not uncommon. Derivation not known.

Gargoyle. A projecting spout to throw the rainwater from the gutter clear of the wall.

Geometrical tracery. (p. 33.)

Groin. The edge formed by the intersection of surfaces in vaulting.

Hagioscope. A squint (which see).

Hammer-beam. (p. 53.)

Header. See Bond.

Hexastyle. A portico with a row of six columns is said to be Hexastyle. [Classic.]

Hip. The angle formed by the intersection of the surfaces of a pyramidal roof. (Fig. 193.)

Hood-mould. The projecting moulding over an arch.

Impost. The horizontal projecting member at the springing of an arch.

Ionic order. (p. 66.)

Jamb. The side of a window or doorway.

King-post. The central vertical post in a roof-truss.

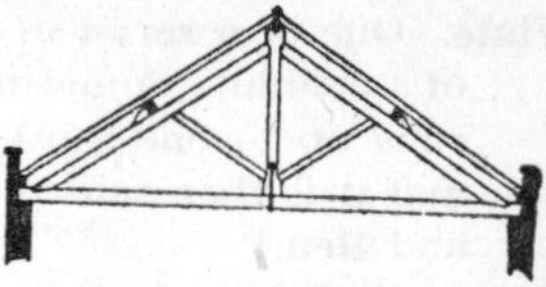

Label. A hood-mould.

FIG. 192

MODERN KING-POST ROOF

Lantern. A timber structure on a roof to admit light or allow the escape of smoke.

Latten. A mixed metal resembling brass.

Lierne vault. (p. 40.)

Louvre. A lantern (*see above*); a sloping board in a lantern or belfry window, arranged so as to allow the passage of air without admitting rain.

Lych-gate. (p. 108).

Machicolations. (pron. makikolations). Small arches carried on corbels to support an overhanging parapet of a castle. There were openings in the gutter so that missiles could be thrown upon assailants.

Mansard Roof. A roof in which the lower part is steep and the central part low pitched.

FIG. 193
A MANSARD ROOF,
HIPPED

Metope. The space between two triglyphs in the frieze of the Doric Order. (p. 64.)

Miserere. A hinged seat in a stall of a church. A bracket was attached to the lower side forming a small secondary seat when the main seat was raised. It was provided for the relief of the infirm during service.

Misericorde. The hall in a monastery in which better fare was allowed than in the frater. (p. 131.)

Mitre. The line formed by the intersection of mouldings or other surfaces, as at the angles of a picture-frame.

Modillion. A bracket under a classical cornice.

Mullion, or Monyal. The vertical division between the lights of a window.

Narthex. A porch extending across the end of an early church. (Fig. 123.)

Newel. The post at the angle of a staircase. The central column of a circular staircase.

Octostyle. A portico with eight columns is said to be Octostyle. [Classic.]

Ogee. A curve composed partly of a convex and partly of a concave line; applied to the sections of mouldings (Fig. 183) and the outlines of arches.

Order. (p. 62.)

Oriel. A bow-window, either corbelled out from the wall or rising from the ground. (p. 58.)

Ovolo. A round convex moulding. (Fig. 197*b*.)

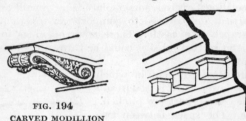

FIG. 194
CARVED MODILLION

FIG. 195
WOOD CORNICE WITH MODILLIONS

Pane. A portion; the term is applied to a window, an alley of a cloister, a side of spire.

Paradise. A garden, courtyard, a cloister garth.

Pargetting. Plaster-work; the term is generally applied to ornamental outside work.

Parlour. (p. 129, and Fig. 163.)

Parvis. (medieval) An enclosure in front of principal door of a church, e.g. St. Paul's.

Patera. A small circular ornament in classical architecture. The term is now often applied to any small carved ornament forming one of a series.

Pediment. A gable in classical architceture.

Peristyle. A colonnade round a courtyard. [Classic.]

Pilaster. A flat, rectangular column against a wall.

Piscina. (p. 110; Fig. 143.)

Plate. A piece of timber lying on a wall to receive rafters, etc.

Plinth. The base of a wall above the ground; the lower part of the base of a column.

Podium. A high plinth or basement-storey. [Classic.]

Poppy-head. A carved finial on the top of a bench-end.

Presbytery. The part of a church in which the high altar stands, east of the choir.

FIG. 196
OGEE ARCH

Pulpitum. (p. 101.)

Purlin. A horizontal timber in a roof resting on the principal rafters and supporting the common rafters. (Fig. 71.)

Quoin. An angle-stone.

FIG. 197
PLAN OF
MULLION:

(a) FILLET;
(b) OVOLO MOULD-
INGS; (c) REBATES

Rebate. A rectangular sinking along the edge of a piece of wood or stone. Sometimes spelt and pronounced 'rabbit'. (Fig. 197.)

Reeded flute. See **Flute.**

Relieving arch. An arch over a lintel.

Respond. A half-column against a wall to receive an arch.

Return. An angle, generally applied to mouldings; thus, in Fig. 77, the hood-mould is said to be returned horizontally at the springing of the arch, and to be returned against the wall. Return-stalls, p. 110.

FIG. 198
PARGETTING.

SCALE:
ABOUT ONE-EIGHTH
OF AN INCH TO
A FOOT

Rubble. Masonry consisting of small irregular stones.

Rustic-work, or **Rustication.** Ashlar masonry with the surface treated in a particular way. There are several varieties: the face of the stone is left rough or is artificially roughened; or it is smooth, but projects and has chamfered or rebated edges. (Fig. 107.)

16

Sacristy. (See **Vestry.**)

Saddle-bar. A horizontal bar of iron in a window.

Sanctus-bell. A bell rung at the consecration of the Host.

Sedilia. Seats for the clergy on the south side of a chancel.

Severy. A bay or compartment of a building.

Shingle. A roof-tile made of split oak.

Soffit. The under side of a cornice, arch, etc.

Solar. (p. 142.)

Spandrel. Applied to almost any surface of irregular form: such as the spaces above an arch; between an arch and a cusp; between the ribs of a vault.

Splay. A large chamfer, as to the jamb of a window, etc.

Squinch. An arch or lintel built across each angle of a tower to form an octagon to carry a spire.

Squint. A hole cut obliquely through the wall of a church to give a view of the high altar.

Stanchion. A vertical iron bar in a window.

Stele. An upright slab of stone sculptured in relief, erected as a memorial to the dead. [Classic.]

Stilted arch. An arch of which the springing is above the capital.

Stoup, or **Stock, Holy-Water-.** A hollow stone near the entrance of a church to contain holy-water.

Strap-work. (p. 57.)

String. A horizontal projecting moulding.

Terra-cotta. Vitrified brick.

Tetrastyle. A portico with a row od four columns is said to be tetrastyle.

Transom. A horizontal division in a window.

Triforium. An upper storey over the aisle of a church.

Triglyph. An ornament in a Doric frieze, consisting of a projection with the two vertical edges chamfered and with two vertical grooves.

Triptych. (pro triptick) A painted panel with two folding-doors, generally used as a reredos.

Tudor flower. An upright leaf used in cresting on the tops of cornices, etc. (Fig. 86.)

Tuscan order. (p. 66.)

Tympanum. The space enclosed (1) between the lintel of a doorway and the relieving arch (Fig. 26), or (2) between the horizontal and curved or sloping cornices of a classical pediment. (Fig. 119.)

Valley. The angle formed by the intersection of two roofs.

Vesica piscis. The pointed oval forming the auriole or glory round representations of the Deity and the Virgin. (Fig. 26.)

Vestry, or **Revestry,** or **Sacristy.** (p. 106.)

Volute. A spiral; the characteristic ornament of the Ionic capital.

Voussoir. An arch-stone.

Wainscot. Panelling on a wall; foreign oak much used for panelling.

Wall-plate. The horizontal timber on which rafters and joists rest.

Wave moulding. A section used in the fourteenth century.

Weathering. A sloping surface of stone, as at the top of a buttress.

FIG. 199
WAVE
MOULDING

Windbrace. A timber springing from the principal rafter, or other member of a roof-truss, to support the purlin and to prevent longitudinal movement in the roof.

Zigzag. A Norman enrichment. (Fig. 25.)

INDEX

TO THE INTRODUCTION, TEXT, AND APPENDIXES

BUT NOT INCLUDED IN THE GLOSSARY

PRINTED BY
JARROLD AND SONS LTD.
NORWICH